PRAISE FOR *SALAD SAMURAI*

"For salad inspiration, I can think of few sources better than the new cookbook *Salad Samurai* . . . Romero brings her fun-loving sensibility and unerring palate to the table. Her recipes, with their brilliant combinations, span the seasons."—**Washington Post**

"Its accessible main course salad recipes are anything but boring, with unexpected flavor combinations that make me wonder—hey, why didn't I think of that?"—**Epicurious.com**

"From one of the most popular vegan cookbook authors of our time comes a collection of perfectly tuned recipes that's long overdue . . . [and that] you don't have to be vegan to love." —**VegNews.com**

"A must for dedicated vegans, a good way to ease into salads for even the most stubborn meat lover, and a great resource for anyone who wants to move to a more sustainable, healthy diet."—**Examiner.com**

"Romero debunks the myth that salads are only an appetizer, using whole food ingredients and plant-based proteins that will appeal to vegans and non-vegans in equal measure . . . a great resource for anyone who wants to move to a more sustainable and healthy diet." —**Philadelphia Tribune**

"Romero is a rock star of vegan cooking. . . . In this book, she shakes up the staid world of salad with her cheeky writing and seasonally arranged salads."—**Portland Press Herald**

PRAISE FOR *VEGANOMICON*

"Spending time with [Moskowitz's] cheerfully politicized book feels like hanging out with Grace Paley. She and her cooking partner, Terry Hope Romero, are as crude and funny when kibbitzing as they are subtle and intuitive when putting together vegan dishes that are full of non-soggy adult tastes."—**New York Times Book Review**

"Exuberant and unapologetic . . . Moskowitz and Romero's recipes don't skimp on fat or flavor, and the eclectic collection of dishes is a testament to the authors' sincere love of cooking and culinary exploration."—**Saveur**

"Full of recipes for which even a carnivore would give up a night of meat."—**San Francisco Chronicle**

"The *Betty Crocker's Cookbook* of the vegan world . . . It's one more step in the quest to prove that vegan food really doesn't taste like cardboard when you know what you're doing." —**BITCH**

ALSO BY TERRY HOPE ROMERO

Salad Samurai

Vegan Eats World

Viva Vegan

WITH ISA CHANDRA MOSKOWITZ

Veganomicon

Vegan Pie in the Sky

Vegan Cookies Invade Your Cookie Jar

Vegan Cupcakes Take Over the World

PROTEIN
NINJA

POWER THROUGH YOUR DAY with 100 HEARTY PLANT-BASED RECIPES THAT PACK A PROTEIN PUNCH

TERRY HOPE ROMERO

Da Capo
LIFE
LONG

A Member of the Perseus Books Group

Copyright © 2016 by Terry Hope Romero
Photos by Vanessa K. Rees

Editorial production by Marrathon Production Services. www.marrathon.net
Designed by Megan Jones Design
Set in 9.5 point Nexa Light

Cataloging-in-Publication data for this book is available from the Library of Congress.

First Da Capo Press edition 2016
ISBN: 978-0-7382-1849-6 (paperback)
ISBN: 978-0-7382-1850-2 (ebook)

Published by Da Capo Press
A Member of the Perseus Books Group
www.dacapopress.com

Da Capo Press books are available at special discounts for bulk purchases in the U.S. by corporations, institutions, and other organizations. For more information, please contact the Special Markets Department at the Perseus Books Group, 2300 Chestnut Street, Suite 200, Philadelphia, PA, 19103, or call (800) 810-4145, ext. 5000, or e-mail special.markets@perseusbooks.com.

10 9 8 7 6 5 4 3 2 1

ENTER THE PROTEIN NINJA

Sneaking vegan proteins into everyday meals and treats.

Unsuspecting whole foods salads, soups, and snacks bumped up to fuel a lifestyle just beyond average activity.

The untrained eye cannot detect the delicate balance of fresh vegetables, wholesome grains, and plant-based proteins in your lunch salad or dinner stew.

Chewy egg- and dairy-free brownies or soft chocolate chip cookies boast the protein content of an egg or a glass of milk.

Comforting breakfast foods—pancakes, waffles, muffins, and even breakfast cookies—don't implode your morning with empty calories but empower you with fiber, fruits, whole grains, and protein.

You've left the realm of ordinary weekday vegan eats. Step into the enclave of *The Protein Ninja*.

*Ninjas are rarely seen, their work done
in the shadows, rarely visible. This goes
out to the staff and volunteer workers
at farm animal sanctuaries everywhere,
whose hard and often unseen work
helps provide a peaceful second life
to countless rescued farm animals.*

CONTENTS

PART 1
ENTER THE PROTEIN NINJA

PART 2
THE RECIPES

BETTER THAN EVER BURGER BOWLS

GRAIN AND NOODLE BOWLS

SWEET TREATS

INTRODUCTION:

THAT OLD PROTEIN QUESTION

Let it be known before you turn the page . . . I know where you get your protein from. And that you're probably doing a decent job of it.

If you eat animal products—meat, dairy, eggs, bugs, don't tell me what else —you're getting enough protein.

If you don't eat any animal products, but your diet is rich in a variety of whole-some plant-based foods—beans, soy foods, nuts and seeds, whole grains, veg-etables and fruits, and even the occasional soy meat, you are also getting enough protein. Probably. Most of the time.

Yet the very existence of this book, *Protein Ninja*, does not imply at all that vegans, vegetarians, or even omnivores who choose to limit their consumption of animal products are not eating enough protein. The seemingly unslayable "But where do you get your protein?" question from well-meaning but frustratingly naive steak-munchers still goads my inner six-teen-year-old vegetarian. To this day. Or occasionally annoys the present day forty-two-year-old vegan typing this sentence.

PROTEIN IS FOR EVERY KIND OF (NON)ATHLETE

About two years ago working out and get-ting in better shape became a priority. Over twenty years of NYC living made an avid walker out of me: Every day can be an urban hike here, if you wear the right shoes and can't afford to cab it everywhere! My interest in weight training came into fo-cus as well: Even in my late teens I flirted with weight lifting, an ungainly fat kid in the YMCA weight room. I've had the same New York Sports Club gym membership since 2001, for crying out loud, and since I joined I've never gone more than two weeks without dropping in for at least a quick spin on the elliptical.

But as I crawl closer to hitting half a century of existence on this beautiful weird planet, I want more from my body. I learned to love weight training, rarely missing a workout. I don't lift on a profes-sional-athlete, leotard-wearing level. Just some weights and plates, barbells and dumbbells, at challenging enough weights to make me sore the next few days in a good way. Enough to begin to see a differ-ence in my body that I liked!

And that's where my interest in sneaking more protein into my diet began. I'm a former chef, a cookbook author, and an avid home cook. I cook after a full day of work (yes, I've usually had other jobs in addition to pounding out endless directions for muffins for over a decade), to unwind and relax. As I started to research what protein foods existed out there for active folks, I wanted protein recipes other than mashing a vanilla-flavored powder with almond butter and chia seeds and calling it a day. I wanted something that really made me feel as if I was cooking. And yes, even good old-fashioned baking! Adding pure, unflavored, but wholesome plant-based protein powders to recipes brings out my inner foodie alchemist.

I heard the call of the protein ninja.

A JOURNEY OF POWDERY PROPORTIONS

Ninjas like strange powders they can blow into the face of enemies to confuse and distract them! So I told myself as I explored the vast and perplexing world of cooking with protein powders.

Yes, we have many plant-based protein sources to choose from besides hemp, rice, and pea-based protein powders: beans, traditional soy foods (tofu, tempeh), "meat" from wheat gluten (seitan), nuts, seeds, even some vegetables and many grains. Much has been written on this subject by people much wiser and more educated than me, and plenty of it is available for free and always at your disposal on the Internet.

Yet sometimes after a tough early-morning weights session, or visiting far-away friends, or long days in the office, or epic bus/plane/train rides to go somewhere fun, or just crawling home after a fifty-minute subway commute that should have been a merciful twenty-eight minutes, it's still a little challenging to fill up on that extra boost of protein from food alone. All too often the "vegan" option on restaurant menus (both fine dining and fast options, and everything in between) consists only of vegetables. No tofu, no mock meats, no nuts: I love vegetables, but I need one or more of these protein sources to feel truly full. And on busy weekdays, filling up on bagels and vending machine pretzels is so much easier than locating a kale chickpea tofu salad.

These recipes are my current answer to the new question "How ELSE will I get my protein?" in the midst of an overbooked life. Booked with fun and important stuff (usually), but still in control of someone who loves food, loves to cook, and would rather spend a little extra time in the kitchen one night for several days of better breakfasts, lunches, snacks, and even dinners.

So, assemble your powders, hide your throwing stars, and button up your *tabi* boots. There's a better way to get better-quality vegan proteins into your daily routine. Are you ready to be a protein ninja?

PART 1

ENTER THE PROTEIN NINJA

STEALTH VEGAN PROTEIN:
A PROTEIN NINJA PRIMER

Plant-based protein powders play a little by their own rules. While they look like flour (sort of), they behave quite unlike flours and have their own unique quirks. The taste and texture of recipes made with them require some getting used to. And you'll just have to go ahead and make some recipes with them, as all the writing in the world can't prepare you. However, I can prepare you with a few essential tips for working with protein powders.

Not every single recipe in this book uses plant-based protein powders, but a lot of them sure do, especially the baked goods. So, please read the following carefully!

PROTEIN POWDERS CHANGE THE TASTE AND TEXTURE OF THINGS

The recipes in this book make tasty waffles, biscuits, cookies, and burgers. But it's worth mentioning that the taste and texture may be a little different than what you're used to.

Pea protein powder has the most pronounced flavor, with mellow chickpealike notes that I think is best suited for savory baked goods and burgers. The texture is perhaps the densest of the three powders.

It's not unlike working with garbanzo bean flour, only with a much finer texture.

When it comes to baked goods that could probably pass for "not swole," a.k.a. your regular friends that would rather wear spandex leggings to a hair metal concert than to the gym, the mild flavor and slightly grainy texture of **brown rice protein powder** wins every time. It's my go-to when I want waffles and biscuits that don't look or taste "healthy," but just hearty. Not unlike brown rice flour, it has a slightly gritty texture.

Hemp protein powder is by far the earthiest of the three and lends a light olive green hue to baked goods, especially those made with light-colored flours. But there's a payoff to that funky hue! It has an appealing nutty flavor and texture, similar to that of finely ground flaxseed, which plays well with a wide range of whole grains and flours, nuts, seeds, and fruits. Not to mention, it can add a boatload of healthful fiber to recipes. Hemp protein has become my go-to protein powder when developing wholesome new recipes. And while I usually opt for unsweetened products, I can get down with lightly sweetened chocolate and vanilla hemp powders.

PROTEIN POWDERS ARE THIRSTY

They may look like flour, but protein powders seem to suck up more liquid than most flours of similar weight and volume. Adding a small portion of dense, moist ingredients—mashed banana, applesauce, beans, pureed winter squash, even mashed sweet potatoes—to a protein-rich baked good or veggie burger provides some much needed moisture and evens out the flavor. Bananas are my favorite in these recipes for their egglike binding properties, but applesauce and cooked winter squash are very helpful.

PROTEIN POWDERS SHOULD BE UNSWEETENED, UNFLAVORED, AND SIMPLE

I buy all kinds of vegan protein powders. Since entering the weekly gym habit of lifting heavy things, I've become an enthusiast of all the interesting meal-replacement, richly flavored, and vitamin-enhanced powders on the market. Chocolate-flavored powders especially have been my friend when I'm traveling and the nutritious vegan options are slim but I know that a powder and my shaker bottle, ice, and some water will help me get through to the next feasible meal.

However, for the majority of recipes in this book (with the exception of, say, the smoothie bowls), use only pure, unflavored, unenriched (that is, no added vitamins) plant-based protein powders.

See the Pantry section for more details, but powders of your concern should be unflavored plain hemp, brown rice, and pea protein. Not only does the neutral flavor of these powders blend well in recipes, but the price point on these is much lower than their high-performance, fancy-flavored cousins.

TRADING POWDERY PLACES

Browsing through the recipes, you'll see that each recipe asks for a particular kind of protein power. Well, one of the three I recommend using: hemp, brown rice, and pea.

These are suggestions only! While I did select the protein powder for each recipe with a particular complementary flavor in mind, you're welcome to try your hand at switching out one for another. In most cases, your muffins will rise, burgers will hold together, waffles will waffle, and so on.

You will notice differences, however: Peek at my notes earlier in the section (well, how DID you get here after all?) and you'll see that hemp protein powder leaves a greenish tinge, brown rice protein powder has a somewhat gritty texture, pea protein is perhaps the densest of the three, and so forth.

If you do switch out and experiment, be smart about it and take notes! Maybe you'll hack these recipes to a new level of greatness. If you do, please let me know!

THE PROTEIN NINJA PANTRY

Having these essential protein- and nutrient-dense ingredients stocked will keep you ready for the next protein ninja mission! Here's a rough shopping list or a general frame of mind for your kitchen. While fresh produce is something you'll buy weekly (sometimes even daily, say, if you love avocados), most of these items can remain fresh for weeks, and in the case of shelf-stable items, months.

The basic protein powders (hemp, brown rice, pea) are becoming commonplace in most natural food stores and even in supplement stores (the ones with posters of heavily oiled-up, tanned weight lifters on the front windows), but now I usually buy mine online for the best value and variety.

REFRIGERATOR

Tofu
It's 2015 and you're probably eating tofu. For this book I use organic tofu of the following kinds: extra firm, firm, and soft. After that there's silken organic tofu, easier to find in shelf-stable aseptic packaging (see Pantry).

Tempeh
Another meatless "meat" substitute workhorse, made from whole soybeans steamed and fermented into a firm (and distinctly non-tofu-like) cake. Opt for whatever tempeh appeals to you most: soy; multigrain; other beans, such as black, chickpea, and adzuki.

Seitan
If you know me or simply my other cookbooks, you know I love steaming seitan when making homemade seitan, as this chewy, hearty "meat" from wheat gluten is easier than making bread. Or go ahead and buy premade seitan; I'll never tell.

PLANT-BASED PROTEIN POWDERS

(best bought in largest size containers for the best value)

- ✘ Unflavored pea protein powder
- ✘ Unflavored brown rice protein powder
- ✘ Unflavored, unsweetened hemp protein powder (any variety, including high fiber, 50% and 70% protein content)
- ✘ Choice of flavored, vitamin-enriched protein powders. For smoothie bowls and some baking, it's best to opt for two basic flavors—chocolate and vanilla—for use in recipes.

Soy, hemp, coconut, or almond milk

Pick your favorite! But still, hands-down, classic soy milk has the most protein for your sipping and cooking buck. I choose soy milks that are just soy, water, and maybe salt, and always unsweetened. Someday I'll make my own at home, but until then I'm chained to the little aseptic box.

White miso

Everybody's favorite fermented soybean condiment! There are many kinds of miso, but white miso plays very well with many flavors and is great in recipes beyond just soup.

Nuts and seeds

Almonds, walnuts, pistachios, cashews, sunflower seeds, chia seeds, shelled hemp seeds, pumpkin seeds (a.k.a. pepitas)—buy them often, buy unroasted, and keep refrigerated in hot months to keep them fresh.

PANTRY

Tofu

Aseptic-packed (sold in shelf-stable cardboard boxes) silken soft tofu. As with anything soy, look for organic, non-GMO varieties.

Nutritional yeast

Every vegan's favorite flaky yellow tasty umami-loaded powder. Found in the bulk bin section or prepacked in bags or jars. PLEASE do not confuse with brewer's yeast, if this is the first time you've ever heard of this ingredient. Make sure to pick up the kind labeled "vegetarian support formula" for all that helpful added vitamin B$_{12}$.

Dried or canned beans

Black, garbanzo, white kidney, and adzuki are some of my favorites.

Whole wheat pastry flour

If you do gluten, whole wheat pastry flour is essential for wholesome and tender muffins, pancakes, scones, and all other nonyeasted breadlike baked goods.

Besan/garbanzo flour

A lovely golden flour made from chickpeas. Essential not just for the gluten-free but great added to baked goods for extra protein and a savory egglike flavor.

Buckwheat flour

Made from guess what? . . . buckwheat! Gluten-free, earthy, delicious. For recipes, I usually blend this dense flour with either some whole wheat flour, or for gluten-free recipes, balance it out with other gluten-free flours.

Dutch-process cocoa powder and natural cocoa powder

These are the two kinds of cocoa powder (and make sure you only buy pure, unsweetened powder for baking). Dutch-processed cocoa powder is more alkaline, darker in hue, and subtler in flavor than the natural stuff. Don't get caught up thinking one is healthier than the other . . . it's still chocolate. If you're already serious about baking, you probably already have both of these. If all you'll ever do is make smoothie bowls, get the natural stuff. If you like to bake, pick up a good-quality organic Dutch-process cocoa, too!

Vital wheat gluten flour

VWGF (okay, nobody calls it that) is a silky flour made only from the protein portion of wheat grains. If you're gluten-free, stop reading here or you might just collapse. If you're not, carry on.

Vital wheat gluten flour was once only used by bakers to enhance bread dough, but for quite some time it's been the ultimate shortcut to making tasty seitan at home. It's also great added to veggie burgers for a special chewy texture and to prevent burgers from crumbling.

Canned coconut milk

By now you probably have at least a few cans of coconut milk in your pantry: Vegan cuisine will forever hold its debt to something once reserved for piña coladas. Coconut milk is commonly available in both light and full-fat versions: for these recipes I use the full-fat version because life is far too short to mess with anything less.

SPECIAL PANTRY GUEST STARS

These ingredients are not exactly basic, yet are a part of many of the recipes in this book. Many are common in natural food stores, and almost everything can be purchased online.

Matcha powder

A style of powdered Japanese green tea with a brilliant green hue and unmistakable bright, grassy finish. Matcha is good for you, too, containing antioxidants just like ordinary green tea. The powder blends easily into recipes for tasty green tea flavored delights.

Maca powder

A powder made from a dried Peruvian root, maca's touted as a superfood with all manner of magical side effects. I'm not going to cite any of them, but I can tell you I like the sweet, maplelike flavor of the powder added to a few foods. It's probably good for you, but the evidence is still being debated. For now, enjoy it in small amounts.

Cacao nibs, chopped

The minimally processed, unsweetened, roasted cacao bean that personally has become my preferred alternative to chocolate chips when making wholesome chocolate baked goods at home. Okay, nobody in their right mind is going to mistake them for chocolate chips, but they have a deep, bittersweet chocolate flavor and crunch enjoyable in many recipes. The most common form is roughly chopped cacao nibs, perfect for using straight out of the bag.

Buckwheat groats

These are the uncracked, uncrushed, unmilled buckwheat grains that I love in granola and other goodies. Look for raw groats, as preroasted have a very heavy flavor that may clash with the recipes in this book.

Agave nectar

I don't use it often, but the supersweet syrup made from a cactuslike agave plant comes in handy in some recipes. As the syrup is used in baked goods loaded with lots of other flavors, you don't need a fancy variety.

Maple syrup

Worth every penny, real maple syrup remains my favorite liquid sweetener. Grade B is perfectly fine for not just cooking and baking, but for sloshing directly onto pancakes and waffles.

Coconut sugar

The newer darling on the natural sweetener market and made from the sap of coconut palms, coconut sugar has a complex caramel flavor not unlike that of light brown sugar. I usually go for the blond (lighter) variety, but experiment with different hues and see what you like best.

Coconut oil

Another food that people insist on laying claim to having magical powers, but really, it's a very nice cooking fat that excels in baked goods, too. Refined coconut oil has had the strong coconut aroma removed. I use both this and virgin coconut oil (packed with rich coconut flavor and aroma) interchangeably, depending on how much coconut flavor I want the end result to have.

NINJA BASICS

For new kitchen ninjas or seasoned kitchen ninjas who want a refresher on the basics, here are a few recipes for staples (beans! grains! coconut bacon! and rockin' seitan!).

COOKING AND FREEZING BEANS

Many of these recipes use beans, so it would be odd to not offer a guide to cooking them at home. Canned beans are fabulous, and in all honestly, I rely on them 90 percent of the time. But between secret ninja missions when I'm just chillin' in the dojo, a pot of homemade beans is a priority.

This is a general guide to making beans! Cooking times can vary a little between the size and shape of beans, but the procedure is the same: soak, drain, boil. That's it! Buy organic ones in bulk from the co-op or in bags in the Latin section of the grocery store; it's all the same cooking game.

Some beans to try cooking at home:

- Black beans
- Chickpeas
- Cannellini beans
- Navy beans
- Pinto beans
- Adzuki beans

The list goes on, but these are the beans I use in this book.

Freezing beans

Freezing beans is easy enough: pack in plastic containers, liquid and all, and freeze solid. To thaw, leave in the refrigerator overnight or drop the container in a pot of hot water for faster thawing. It's helpful to pack beans in smaller, 2-cup containers for speedy thawing.

COOKING AND FREEZING GRAINS

Grains are pretty easy to cook; the basics follow. If you can cook grains in your sleep, you are a better ninja than I! If you're on a secret mission and need some right away, the freezer is your friend.

Freezing brown rice or quinoa

Now that you've cooked some brown rice, you see that while super tasty, it's not exactly the fastest-cooking food on the shelf.

While some upscale organic markets carry frozen brown rice, you can make your own at a fraction of the cost and be prepared like a ninja for any surprise stir-fry attack.

1. Let the cooked brown rice or quinoa cool for 20 minutes, or until cool enough to handle.

2. Have ready a baking sheet that fits into your freezer and resealable plastic

freezer bags; the 2-cup size is ideal for easy to use "single" servings of cooled grain.

3. Measuring the cooled grain into equal-size portions is your friend. Lightly wet a 1-cup measuring cup and wet your hands. Scoop and measure the cooled grain, pour it into the bag, and gently flatten the bag so that the grain is an even layer about an inch thick. Press as much air out of the bag as possible and seal.

4. Layer the bags onto the cookie sheet and freeze. If possible, arrange in single layer for the fastest freezing. When the grain is frozen solid, reclaim that cookie sheet (and make cookies!) and use that frozen rice or quinoa within 2 months for best flavor.

PRO-TIP: *This technique also works for freezing other cooked grains.*

SAVORY STAPLES

The following two recipes are for savory vegan staples you can find in many Whole Foods or similar well-stocked natural food markets. BUT these are also simple things to make at home.

RECIPE ICONS AND THIS BOOK

The following icons show at a glance which protein (or mix of proteins) is in each recipe.

 GF   Gluten-free

 SF   Soy-free

 VPP   Vegan protein powder (use your favorite flavored, fortified vegan protein powder: Raw Fit, Vega, etc.)

 PPP   Pea protein powder

 HPP   Hemp protein powder

 BRP   Brown rice protein powder

 SP   Soy protein (tofu or tempeh)

 LP   Legume protein (beans other than soy or pea protein powder)

 WP   Wheat protein (made with vital wheat gluten. Stay away, GF people!)

NSP   Nut/seed protein (any seed and any nut, even peanuts, which are technically a legume)

BASIC BEAN RECIPE

MAKES: 4-6 CUPS BEANS
TIME: 2-2½ HOURS, NOT INCLUDING SOAKING TIME

1 pound dried beans

1 teaspoon salt

2 bay leaves

1 Spread the beans on a large, clean work surface. Pick and discard any debris or broken beans.

2 Transfer the beans to a large bowl, cover with at least 6 inches of water, and set aside on the countertop to soak overnight or for 8 to 10 hours. If you want to cook the beans after work, set the beans to soak before you leave the house in the morning.

3 For speed soaking, boil the unsoaked beans in plain, fresh cold water for 5 minutes over high heat. Turn off the heat, partially cover, and let the beans just soak and hang out for 1 hour. Proceed as directed.

4 Drain the beans and rinse thoroughly with fresh cold water. Pour the beans into a large soup pot and cover with 8 cups of cold water. Add the salt and bay leaves. Bring to a rolling boil over high heat for 5 minutes, then lower the heat to low. Partially cover and simmer the beans for another 1½ to 2½ hours.

5 The beans are ready when they are very tender: Scoop up a few beans, taste, and if you can easily crush them with your tongue, they're ready! Don't consume "crunchy" undercooked beans, unless you love rumbly tummies. Remember: A gassy ninja is not a stealthy ninja.

6 Let the beans cool in their liquid for about 30 minutes before packing (along with their liquid) into containers. Refrigerate and use within a week, or freeze!

QUINOA

MAKES: 3 CUPS COOKED QUINOA
TIME: 25 MINUTES OR LESS

My approach toward cooking everyone's favorite high-protein, quick-cooking, crunchy, and versatile gluten-free grain is really not so different than standard methods. But I do find that toasting the quinoa before cooking adds some extra flavor.

1 Toast the quinoa in a large, dry saucepan over medium-high heat for 3 to 4 minutes, stirring frequently, until the grain is fragrant.

2 Pour in the water or vegan broth, increase the heat to high, and bring to a rolling boil. Boil for a minute, lower the heat to low, and stir a few times. Cover the pan and cook for 20 minutes, or until the liquid is absorbed.

3 Fluff the quinoa with a fork and serve hot! Or chill the quinoa for 30 minutes or overnight if using in a stir-fry.

1 cup uncooked white, red, or black quinoa (or a blend of colors)

1¾ cups water or vegan vegetable broth

¼ teaspoon salt (omit if using a flavorful vegan broth)

SHORT-GRAIN BROWN RICE

MAKES: ABOUT 4 CUPS RICE
TIME: ABOUT 1 HOUR

1 In a large saucepan, bring the rice, water, and salt to a rolling boil over high heat. Boil for 5 minutes, then lower the heat to low.

2 Stir the rice once, then tightly cover. Simmer the rice for 40 to 45 minutes, or until all the water has been absorbed. Turn off the heat, keep covered, and let stand for 5 minutes. Fluff and serve!

1 cup uncooked short-grain brown rice

2 cups water

Big pinch of salt

THE STEAMED SEITAN TO RULE THEM ALL

MAKES: ABOUT 32 OUNCES SEITAN

1½ cups cold, richly flavored vegan vegetable broth

2 garlic cloves, minced or grated with a Microplane grater

3 tablespoons soy sauce or coconut aminos (for soy-free seitan)

1¾ cups vital wheat gluten flour, or 1 (10-ounce) package

⅓ cup garbanzo bean or black bean flour

¼ cup nutritional yeast

1 teaspoon ground cumin or dried thyme

¼ cup olive oil

Seitan, that clever "meat from wheat," still brings on the questions: What is it, what do you do with it . . . how do you pronounce it ("SAY-tan")? Let it be a mystery no longer! If you can knead dough, you can make this (it's far simpler than making bread).

These rustic cutlets are the easiest version of the ultra-simple steamed seitan I've been making for years, but you can bake them for a dense chewy texture. Either way, just mix, wrap, and cook for a succulent, handmade veggie protein that loves marinades and is great on the grill for a "meaty" salad topping.

1 In a 1-quart glass measuring cup or bowl, whisk together the vegetable broth, garlic, and soy sauce. In a separate bowl, stir together the vital wheat gluten, garbanzo bean flour, nutritional yeast, and cumin or thyme. Form a well in the center and pour in the olive oil, and use your fingers or a fork to work the oil in until the mixture looks sandy. Pour in the broth mixture.

2 Stir with a rubber spatula; when all of the broth has been absorbed and the mixture pulls away from the sides of the bowl, use both hands to knead the mixture for a minute. For the best texture results, knead the mixture in one direction, using a folding and pressing motion with your palms. Let the mixture rest for 10 minutes, then use a knife to cut it into four equal pieces.

3 Tear off two 10-inch-long pieces of foil. In the center of
each piece of foil, pat each piece of the mixture into a
thin oval less than ½ inch thick. Now seal each packet for
steaming: Bring the long edges of the foil together and
fold together with a seam about ¼ inch wide, then fold
another seam, and press together to seal tightly; there
should be some space under this little foil tent above the
seitan inside. Tightly crimp the opposite ends; the end
result should be a loose foil pouch with tightly sealed
seams. The seitan will expands as it steams, so make sure
you have some room left over in the foil pouch! Repeat
with remaining seitan portions.

4 Set up your steamer and steam the seitan for 25
minutes. Take care that the seitan does not touch the
water. The loaves will expand and feel firm when done;
if not, continue to steam for another 5 minutes. Remove
the seitan from the steamer and let cool on the kitchen
counter for 20 minutes before using, or store in a tightly
covered container in the refrigerator for up to a week. For
best flavor and texture, let the seitan cool to room temperature, then chill overnight. If desired, freeze the seitan
and use within 2 months; to defrost, leave in the refrigerator overnight.

5 To bake the seitan, heat it in a preheated 350°F oven
for 30 minutes. Let cool and store as directed above.
Make sure to leave room in the foil pouches even if you're
baking seitan; it will expand during baking, too!

MY BEST COCONUT BACON

MAKES: ABOUT 2 CUPS BACON

2 tablespoons pure maple syrup

2 tablespoons tamari

1 tablespoon all-natural tomato ketchup

1 tablespoon liquid smoke

2 cups large, unsweetened coconut flakes

If there's one hot-ticket vegan munchable you can make right now that will add vast amounts of excitement to not just any recipe in this book, but any recipe you make ever for the remainder of your sweet and whimsical life, it's coconut bacon.

Or more simply put, you need smoky, crispy bits of bacony coconut. And even better, it's easy enough to make at home.

1 Preheat the oven to 325°F and line a large baking sheet with parchment paper.

2 In a large mixing bowl, whisk together all the ingredients, except the coconut. Pour in the coconut and use a rubber spatula to thoroughly stir and completely coat the flakes in the sauce.

3 Spread the flakes in a thin layer on the parchment paper and roast for 20 to 25 minutes, stirring occasionally. Watch carefully to avoid burning. Let cool completely before storing in an airtight container and store in a dark, cool place. For best results use within 1 week, if not poured over everything you eat in the next 24 hours, that is.

PRO-TIP: For superior results, use only large flakes of unsweetened coconut. Tasty but less visually appealing is finely grated, desiccated coconut. But never use the sweet, sugary, soggy stuff typically found in regular grocery stores.

PART 2

THE

RECIPES

UNSTOPPABLE SMOOTHIE BOWLS and GRANOLA

My affair with smoothie bowls started out innocently enough. The once-a-week blending of a few frozen bananas with a dash of soy milk for "ice cream"[1] as an after-dinner treat turned risqué when I craved it for breakfast. After all, blended banana with just enough liquid for a thick, creamy consistency you can eat with a spoon is just a smoothie, right? A smoothie beyond the glass. A smoothie that requires a bowl.

I added my daily portion of protein powder to blended banana and enjoyed it before I even got in the shower. One morning became the next, and it became clear there was no going back. It became too easy to load the smoothie bowl with a layer of crunchy granola. (And my escalating granola consumption's contributing to Big Granola made me change course, stop buying granola, and make my own at home. A good thing, you gotta agree.) Next up: any fresh fruit or even gently thawed frozen berries. Goji berries? Hell, yes. Cacao nibs . . . melted peanut butter . . . get the fuck out! I was hooked on protein-laced "ice cream" for breakfast. Usually with hot black coffee, or green tea on gentler days.

I vowed to make my last smoothie bowl of the season in late November (pumpkin spice 4 ever) . . . only to go back on my promise a few weeks later well into winter. Most likely something with chocolate and almonds. I buckle when you wave that combo in my face.

Almost a year later, I'm not ashamed to admit I'm hooked. I will always love the usual breakfast foods. (I mean, look at the table of contents of this book: It's a stampede of pancakes, scones, and toasts.) But when it comes to getting away with being a grown up and getting an extra boost of protein after a workout AND eating freakin' "ice cream" first thing in the morning, it's the smoothie bowl life for me.

---

[1] "Ice cream" is in quotes for all of those who feel their blood pressure rise when someone calls a smooshed frozen banana ice cream. I'm well aware that a blended banana is not the same as a carefully crafted vegan ice cream recipe made, for example, with cashew or coconut milk. Now, be off and go make yourself something sweet and healthy for a breakfast, snack, or completely responsible grown-up dinner-dessert.

RUSH HOUR

Smoothie bowls fire away at the speed of a blender. Faster than a pancake or a bowl of oatmeal!

Yet there are some mornings when even chopping and blending steal away precious minutes. In that instance, assembling and freezing a few bowls in advance makes the difference.

Here's a few tips for smoothie bowl on-the-go success:

- Pack each serving of a smoothie bowl into a small individual plastic container. A 24-ounce (3-cup) container is the perfect size for easy thawing.

- Store crunchy toppings (granola, toasted nuts) in separate small containers and add just before eating.

- Smoothie bowls thaw easily at normal room temperatures. If it's a bit cold, heat the container in a bowl of warm water for a few minutes.

LET'S TALK FROZEN FRUIT

There's really no other way to say it, so I'm going to be blunt: You need to stock your freezer full of all kinds of frozen fruits to live the ballin' lifestyle of a smoothie bowl ninja master.

Do it often, do it weekly. Keep tabs on what's in the freezer so you don't have tragic mornings without a smoothie bowl when you need it most. Lest you end up . . . drinking your protein powder in a boring almond milk smoothie instead. Gasp!

Depending on where you live and your access to fresh produce, you may scoff when I tell you that I buy big bags of frozen raspberries, blueberries, and strawberries weekly. (If you happen to live in a year-round futuristic bio-dome where organic heirloom berries and avocados tumble onto your doorstep every morning, I salute you. Proceed to the recipes.)

I live in New York City, whose climate is not known for its rich abundance or variety of local produce all year round. I live in a dim apartment without a fire escape for a baby banana tree. And I must have my smoothie bowls weekly! Therefore I will keep the purses of those frozen fruit barons bulging for many years to come. Here are some of my favorite fruits I keep stashed in the freezer:

Bananas

Couldn't be any easier. I usually buy an extra bunch and freeze them all together. Before you chuck them on ice, allow your bananas to ripen considerably (a few brown spots are good) for the sweetest bowls. Peel, don't slice, and pack into resealable plastic freezer bags or plastic containers.

Frozen banana tips:

- Always use frozen bananas right after removing from the freezer. If you allow them to thaw completely, they become a pathetic puddle of mucus (sorry, true) and not the creamy sweet ambrosia they once were.

- Experiment with slicing or breaking into a few pieces beforehand. If you have the freezer space, perhaps freeze each piece separately on a waxed paper–lined baking sheet before packing up. BUT I find I spend the same amount of time slicing apart frozen slices as I do just cutting up a whole frozen banana, so I never bother slicing or breaking up bananas. But that's how I live my life. You just have to try it for yourself and see what works best for you.

Avocado

If you haven't been freezing avocado already, get ready for your life to seriously change. Start with ripe Haas avocado (fatty avocado varieties work best here), slice in half, peel, and discard or do something else with the pit. Slice the avocado halves into three or four wedges, arrange on a parchment paper–lined tray, and freeze solid. Store the frozen wedges in airtight containers in, you guessed it, the freezer.

Unlike using frozen banana, it's easiest to work with frozen avocado if it has been allowed to thaw just ever so slightly. Depending on the room temperature, it can be a minute or as many as four. Slice into small chunks when it's just about soft enough and blend right away.

Berries

I confess: I usually buy mine already frozen. But if I find myself with a bumper crop of fresh blueberries or cherries (one of those things with a short growing season), I will go to town. I wash, dry very well, remove any pits (cherries, looking at you), then spread in a baking pan and freeze. After they freeze solid, they get packed up in resealable plastic freezer bags.

Make use of your grocery store's freezer. Here's what I buy frozen all the time:

- Açai puree packets
- Acerola cherry packets
- Blackberries
- Blueberries
- Frozen kale, when available
- Frozen spinach
- Mangoes (so easy! No peeling, no pits, in cubes ready to go)
- Pineapple (tasty and mess-free compared to fresh)
- Raspberries
- Strawberries
- Tropical fruit purees of the sort Goya makes: passion fruit, guanabana, tamarind, mora (Andean blackberry), etc.

MANGO AVOCADO HEMP SMOOTHIE BOWL

MAKES: 1 SERVING
TIME: LESS THAN 10 MINUTES

1 cup diced frozen mango

½ frozen banana

¼ frozen Haas avocado, slightly thawed

⅓ cup unsweetened vanilla or plain coconut milk (from a carton, not canned)

¼ cup pure or flavored hemp protein powder

1 teaspoon coconut sugar (optional)

½ teaspoon pure vanilla extract

Refreshing and tropical, this creamy, cool breakfast treat will transport you into a song. (It might be a Jimmy Buffett song, YIKES. You've been warned.) Unflavored hemp protein works great in this recipe, but you can use your favorite vegan vanilla protein powder in its place. If you do, leave out the coconut sugar and vanilla extract.

1 Pulse all the ingredients in a blender on low to medium speed. Occasionally stop blending and use a rubber spatula to scrape down the sides.

2 The idea is to pulse only enough to blend everything into a thick, creamy mass, a little bit like soft-serve ice cream. Take care not to overblend or blend at too high a speed, as the resulting heat will melt the smoothie bowl.

3 When blended and smooth, scoop into a bowl, add your favorite toppings, and eat immediately!

MATCHA MINT BOWL

Blend in 1 teaspoon of matcha tea powder and a handful of fresh mint leaves.

AÇAI AVOCADO BOWL

Replace the frozen mango with two (100 g) packets of açai, slightly thawed. If you came here for an açai bowl, your search is over.

PAPAYA LIME BOWL

Replace the frozen mango with frozen papaya and blend in 2 tablespoons of freshly squeezed lime juice.

VANILLA ALMOND SMOOTHIE BOWL

1 heaping cup sliced frozen banana (about 1½ whole bananas)

1 scoop (about ¼ cup) of your favorite vegan protein powder, unflavored or vanilla

⅓ cup vanilla unsweetened almond milk

1 tablespoon almond butter

1 teaspoon chia seeds

Dash (about ⅛ teaspoon) of almond or pure vanilla extract

MAKES: 1 SERVING
TIME: LESS THAN 10 MINUTES

Vanilla gets a bad rap for meaning "tame, ordinary, or uncreative, boring, dull, uninspired . . . Anyway, where was I? This creamy and smooth frosty breakfast bowl is delightful the way it is. Or use it as a building block: Load it up with seasonal fruit, any kind of granola, nuts, crumbled cookies. Or go ahead, and just follow the recipe; it may be plain, but it ain't boring.

1 Pulse all the ingredients in a blender on low to medium speed. Occasionally stop blending and use a rubber spatula to scrape down the sides.

2 The idea is to pulse only enough to blend everything into a thick, creamy mass, a little bit like soft-serve ice cream. Take care not to overblend or blend at too high a speed, as the resulting heat will melt the smoothie bowl.

3 When blended and smooth, scoop into a bowl, add your favorite toppings, and eat immediately!

A journey of a thousand smoothie bowls starts with a few variations:

PEANUT BUTTER STRAWBERRY BOWL

Replace the almond butter with peanut butter. Pulse in two or three frozen strawberries. Top the bowl with either slightly thawed frozen strawberries or raspberries and 1 tablespoon of melted peanut butter whisked with 1 teaspoon of pure maple syrup. For an equally flavorful and less fatty treat, try this with your favorite flavor of powdered peanut butter.

GINGER CHAI SPICE BOWL

Blend in 1 tablespoon of grated fresh ginger or ½ teaspoon of ground ginger, ½ teaspoon of ground cinnamon, and a pinch each of ground cloves and ground cardamom. Sprinkle more ground cinnamon on top.

MATCHA LATTE BOWL

Blend in 1 teaspoon of pure matcha green tea powder. Sprinkle a little extra matcha powder on top.

PUMPKIN PIE BOWL

Blend in ¼ cup of cooked, chilled pumpkin puree (fresh or canned), 1 tablespoon of grated fresh ginger or ½ teaspoon of ground, ½ teaspoon of ground cinnamon, and a pinch of freshly grated nutmeg. Sprinkle your favorite cinnamon spice granola and extra ground cinnamon on top.

CHOCOLATE AVOCADO SMOOTHIE BOWL

MAKES: 1 SERVING
TIME: LESS THAN 10 MINUTES

This deep, rich, velvety bowl made even creamier with frozen avocado enjoyed in the morning could change your whole day: You'll find a twenty-dollar bill on the ground, make friends with pit bulls, or catch every train for the perfect commute to work. Or you could just pretend you're eating chocolate soft-serve ice cream for this ultrawholesome breakfast.

1 Pulse all the ingredients in a blender on low to medium speed. Occasionally stop blending and use a rubber spatula to scrape down the sides.

2 The idea is to pulse only enough to blend everything into a thick, creamy mass, a little bit like soft-serve ice cream. Take care not to overblend or blend at too high a speed, as the resulting heat will melt the smoothie bowl.

3 When blended and smooth, scoop into a bowl, add your favorite toppings, and eat immediately!

continued ➲

1 heaping cup sliced frozen banana (about 1½ whole bananas)

½ Haas avocado, frozen, pitted, peeled, and sliced

1 scoop (about ¼ cup) of your favorite vegan protein powder, unflavored, vanilla, or chocolate

½ cup vanilla almond milk or pure coconut water

2 large, soft dates, pitted

2 tablespoons raw or high-quality cocoa powder

2 teaspoons chia seeds

¼ teaspoon pure vanilla extract

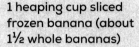

CHOCOLATE ALMOND BOWL

Blend in ¼ teaspoon of almond extract and stir in ¼ cup of chopped roasted almonds.

MOCHA BOWL

Blend in either 1 teaspoon of espresso powder OR 1 chilled shot of home-brewed espresso.

COLD BREW BOMBER BOWL

Replace half, or if you're ready to lose your mind, ALL of the almond milk with cold brewed coffee.

CHOCOLATE MINTY GREENS BOWL

Fresh remix: Blend in ½ cup of chopped kale or spinach greens plus a handful of fresh mint.

Pantry remix: Out of fresh green leafy stuff? Use 1 scoop of your favorite powdered greens plus ¼ teaspoon of mint extract.

PINEAPPLE YOGURT BOWL

MAKES: 1 SERVING
TIME: LESS THAN 10 MINUTES

One cannot live on chocolate or vanilla alone! Presenting that perfectly fruity smoothie bowl with the added benefit of probiotics from a scoop of vegan yogurt. Not a fan of vegan yogurt? Check out the kefir water and coconut milk alternative for a blast of creamy flavor and probiotic power.

1 Pulse all the ingredients in a blender on low to medium speed. Occasionally stop blending and use a rubber spatula to scrape down the sides.

2 The idea is to pulse only enough to blend everything into a thick, creamy mass, a little bit like soft-serve ice cream. Take care not to overblend or blend at too high a speed, as the resulting heat will melt the smoothie bowl.

3 When blended and smooth, scoop into a bowl, add your favorite toppings, and eat immediately!

continued ➲

1 large frozen banana, chopped

½ cup frozen pineapple, chopped

1 scoop or serving of your favorite vegan protein powder, plain, vanilla, or berry-flavored

¼ cup unsweetened plain or vanilla almond or hemp milk

¼ cup vanilla or lemon vegan yogurt (almond, coconut, or soy based)

ACEROLA CHERRY VITAMIN C MONSTER BOWL

Add 1 (100 g) packet of frozen acerola cherry pulp. Thaw slightly before blending. This will be tart, which I love, but if you want to sweeten it up, add a drizzle of pure maple syrup or agave nectar as it blends.

GINGER LEMON CAYENNE COLD BLASTER BOWL

This is a great bowl all year round when you're feeling a little under the weather or you are doing some kind of cleanse, if you're into that kind of thing. It's wonderfully comforting if you're stricken by a dreadful summer cold!

Add 1 tablespoon of freshly squeezed lemon juice, 1 tablespoon of grated fresh ginger, and ½ teaspoon of ground turmeric to the mixture before blending. Sprinkle the top of the finished smoothie bowl with ¼ to ½ teaspoon of cayenne pepper if you're crazy like me, or blend it in for a smoother consistency.

WATERMELONBERRY BOWL

Omit the banana and substitute 2 cups of diced, seedless watermelon. Instead of the pineapple, use frozen diced strawberries or raspberries. Sweeten with agave nectar or pure maple syrup to taste.

PRO-TIP: *If you can get your hot little hands on some kefir water—a dairy-free cultured beverage made with water and sweetener—use this in place of the vegan yogurt for a dose of probiotic goodness in your gut. And if you're not a fan of kefir water? Coconut water to the rescue. You can use the straight-up, just-coconut stuff, or fruit-flavored for additional sweetness.*

CHOCOLATE MACA CHIA PUDDING

HPP   NSP

MAKES: 1 PINT
TIME: LESS THAN 10 MINUTES

Little-known fact: Our insatiable hunger for chia seed puddings has now put the world's Chia Pet population on the endangered species list. So, if you're gonna eat chia, live it up and why not power boost that strange yet ever-so-tasty treat with a raw cacao, cacao nibs, and chocolaty hemp protein.

1 Pour into a pint-size mason jar the almond milk, hemp protein powder, cocoa powder, maca powder, vanilla, and cinnamon. Seal the jar tightly and shake vigorously until the mixture is smooth. Alternatively, you can pulse everything together in a blender, then pour into the jar.

2 Add the chia seeds and cacao nibs, seal the jar again, and shake until well blended. Chill for an hour, or even better, overnight, for the best flavor and texture.

1 cup unsweetened vanilla or chocolate almond milk

¼ cup chocolate hemp protein powder

1 tablespoon raw cocoa powder

1 tablespoon maca powder

¼ teaspoon pure vanilla extract

Pinch of ground cinnamon

3 tablespoons raw chia seeds

1 tablespoon chopped cacao nibs

STRAWBERRY 'N' PROTEIN CHIA PUDDING

HPP NSP

MAKES: 1 PINT PUDDING
TIME: LESS THAN 10 MINUTES

- ¾ cup unsweetened almond or soy milk
- ¼ cup canned full-fat coconut milk
- 1 cup sliced frozen or fresh strawberries
- ¼ cup unflavored pea protein powder
- 1 tablespoon maca powder
- 1 tablespoon freshly squeezed lemon juice
- 1 tablespoon pure maple syrup
- ¼ teaspoon pure vanilla extract
- ¼ teaspoon strawberry extract (optional)
- ¼ cup chia seeds

With its fresh and delicate flavors, this one screams "summer." If you want even more summer—and a bigger strawberry flavor—say, in the middle of winter, consider a touch of strawberry extract. The coconut milk (use the canned stuff here) adds an insane creaminess.

1 Pour into a pint-size mason jar the almond milk, coconut milk, strawberries, pea protein powder, maca powder, lemon juice, maple syrup, vanilla, and strawberry extract, if using. Seal the jar tightly and shake vigorously until the mixture is smooth. Alternatively, you can pulse everything together in a blender, then pour into the jar.

2 Add the chia seeds, seal the jar again, and shake until well blended. Chill for an hour, or even better, overnight, for the best flavor and texture.

ANY BERRY PROTEIN CHIA PUDDING
Replace the strawberries with raspberries or blueberries. Raspberries create the sharpest, cleanest flavor out of the three-berry triad that rules everything around me.

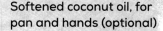

CHOCOLATE HAZELNUT HEMP GRANOLA

⬥ GF   ⬥ HPP   ✦ NSP

MAKES: ABOUT 6 CUPS GRANOLA
TIME: LESS THAN 10 MINUTES

Ah, chocolate and hazelnuts. Truly, there is no finer combination. It makes chocolate and peanut butter taste like raw eggplant and canned refried beans. Okay, not really, I love PB&C, but if I thought my editor would let me, I'd work chocolate and hazelnut into every recipe (editor's note: next book). Luckily for everyone, granola turns out to be the perfect vehicle for Nutella-like goodness. Enriched with hemp protein, a handful of this munchy treat has helped get me through many a busy day.

1 Preheat the oven to 325°F. Lightly oil two 9 x 13-inch baking pans with coconut oil, or line with parchment paper.

2 In a large mixing bowl, combine the oats, buckwheat, chia seeds, and hemp protein powder. In a small mixing bowl, whisk together the maple syrup, molasses, cocoa powder, coconut oil, vanilla, cinnamon, and salt into a thick syrup.

3 Pour the liquid mixture over the oat mixture and add the hazelnuts. Use a rubber spatula to not only mix the liquid mixture with the oat mixture, but to firmly mash it into the oats and nuts and completely coat everything. Alternatively, lightly coat your hands with a little coconut oil and knead the syrup into the oats and nuts. Spread in

continued ➲

Softened coconut oil, for pan and hands (optional)

4 cups old-fashioned rolled oats

1 cup buckwheat groats

2 tablespoons chia seeds

⅓ cup hemp protein powder

¼ cup pure maple syrup

2 tablespoons organic molasses

3 tablespoons raw cocoa powder

3 tablespoons coconut oil, melted

½ teaspoon pure vanilla extract

½ teaspoon ground cinnamon

½ teaspoon salt

1 cup whole hazelnuts, roughly chopped

3 tablespoons cacao nibs

½ cup dried cherries (optional . . . or are they?)

an even layer into the prepared pans and roast for 35 to 45 minutes, stirring occasionally, or until the oats are crisp and have a glossy sheen to them and the hazelnuts are lightly toasted.

4 Remove the granola from the oven. Add the cacao nibs and cherries and stir into the hot granola; the heat will help lightly steam the fruit. Let the granola cool completely before storing in airtight containers. Eat within 3 weeks for the biggest, best flavor.

MOCHA LATTE GRANOLA

Whisk 2 tablespoons of espresso powder into the maple syrup mixture.

CHOCOLATE GINGERBREAD GRANOLA

Whisk 1 tablespoon of ground ginger into the maple syrup mixture and increase the ground cinnamon to 1½ teaspoons.

TRAIL MIX PROTEIN GRANOLA

PPP   NSP

MAKES: ABOUT 6 CUPS GRANOLA
TIME: LESS THAN 10 MINUTES

Even granola haters would dig this soft and chewy granola, chock-full of fruits, seeds, nuts, and gently toasted grains. Every wholesome bite will send you packing for the great outdoors, but don't worry, this pea protein–enriched granola will surely save your life someday when you're lost in the woods. But please don't get lost in the woods.

1 Preheat the oven to 325°F. Lightly oil two 9 x 13 inch baking pans with coconut oil, or line with parchment paper.

2 In a large mixing bowl, combine the oats, quinoa flakes, buckwheat groats, almonds, sunflower seeds, pepitas, hemp seeds, and pea protein powder. In a small mixing bowl, thoroughly whisk together the olive oil, agave nectar, orange juice, vanilla, and salt.

3 Pour the liquid mixture over the oat mixture. Use a rubber spatula to not only mix the liquid mixture with the oat mixture, but to firmly mash it into the grains and nuts and completely coat everything. Spread in an even layer into the prepared pans and roast for 35 to 45 minutes, stirring occasionally, or until the oats are dry and the nuts and seeds are lightly toasted.

4 Remove the granola from the oven. Add the raisins and blueberries and stir into the hot granola; the heat will help lightly steam the fruit. Let the granola cool completely before storing in airtight containers. Eat within 3 weeks for the biggest, best flavor.

Softened coconut oil, for pan (optional)

3 cups old-fashioned rolled oats

2 cups quinoa flakes, crispy brown rice cereal, or additional old-fashioned rolled oats

1 cup raw buckwheat groats

½ cup whole almonds or peanuts

½ cup sunflower seeds

½ cup raw pepitas

¼ cup shelled hemp seeds

⅔ cup unflavored pea protein powder

⅓ cup olive oil

½ cup dark agave nectar

½ cup freshly squeezed orange juice

1 teaspoon pure vanilla extract

½ teaspoon salt

½ cup organic dark raisins

½ cup organic dried blueberries or cranberries

MATCHA STRAWBERRY GRANOLA

HPP NSP

Softened coconut oil, for pan and hands (optional)

3 cups old-fashioned rolled oats

3 cups crispy brown rice cereal

1 cup sliced almonds

3 tablespoons chia seeds

½ cup unflavored hemp protein powder

½ cup pure maple syrup

¼ cup coconut oil, melted

2 tablespoons pure unsweetened matcha powder

1 teaspoon pure vanilla extract

½ teaspoon almond extract

½ teaspoon salt

½ cup freeze-dried strawberries

MAKES: ABOUT 8 CUPS GRANOLA
TIME: LESS THAN 10 MINUTES

I'm here to tell you that matcha green tea, a touch of almond flavor, and the bright crunchy notes from freeze-dried strawberries makes for a gorgeous green granola that will fill your kitchen with the soothing aromas of green tea, coconut, and vanilla!

1 Preheat the oven to 325°F. Lightly oil two 9 x 13 inch baking pans with coconut oil, or line with parchment paper.

2 In a large mixing bowl, combine the oats, crispy brown rice, almonds, chia seeds, and hemp protein powder. In a small mixing bowl, thoroughly whisk together the maple syrup, melted coconut oil, matcha powder, vanilla, almond extract, and salt into a thick syrup.

3 Pour the liquid mixture over the oat mixture. Use a rubber spatula to not only mix the liquid mixture with the oat mixture, but to firmly mash it into the grains and nuts and completely coat everything. Spread in an even layer into the prepared pans and roast for 35 to 45 minutes, stirring occasionally, or until the oats are crisp and have a glossy sheen to them, and the almonds are lightly toasted.

4 Remove the granola from the oven. Let the granola cool completely before stirring in the freeze-dried strawberries and storing in airtight containers. Best if consumed within 1 month.

PRO-TIP: *Freeze-dried strawberries are my favorite here, but substituting dried cranberries or cherries works just fine here, too. Instead of waiting for the granola to cool, stir the dried fruit into warm granola to soften it up a bit.*

STEALTHY PROTEIN PANCAKES, WAFFLES, *and* MUCH MUCH MORE

You don't have to be a morning person to love breakfast for dinner, brunch, lunch, trunch, linner, second breakfast, or any other made-up and completely brilliant excuse to eat pancakes or waffles any time of day or night.

Unless you've been living under a yoga mat the past few years, protein-loaded pancakes, waffles, and breakfast foods are trendy! I'm about as trendy as a fanny pack, but I love breakfast foods not just for breakfast. (Pumping waffle irons is the next hot workout, if you ask me.) As I've shifted gears to eat more vegetables, I want my favorite pancake or waffle-shaped delivery method for carbs to include a little extra protein.

Nearly all of these recipes, from sausages to waffles to pancakes, are easy to make in big batches and freeze. No more overpriced, empty-calorie breakfast cereals for you! Woman and man cannot live on pancakes alone (and I've tried), so there's biscuits and gravy, tempeh bacon, and Indian-inspired gluten-free *pudla* to shake up that protein breakfast routine.

EVERYDAY PEA PROTEIN PANCAKES

PPP

⅓ cup unflavored pea or brown rice protein powder

1½ cups unsweetened plain or vanilla soy or almond milk

¼ cup water

½ cup mashed ripe banana (about 1 small banana) or unsweetened applesauce

1 tablespoon apple cider vinegar

1 tablespoon canola or olive oil

¾ cup unbleached all-purpose flour

⅔ cup whole wheat pastry flour

1 tablespoon coconut sugar

1 tablespoon baking powder

½ teaspoon salt

Cooking oil spray or canola oil, for griddle

Frozen or fresh blueberries, or walnuts (optional)

MAKES: ABOUT 10 (5-INCH) PANCAKES
TIME: LESS THAN 30 MINUTES

Sometimes you need simple but good-for-you whole-grain pancakes. It could be on the weekend like regular people, but if you're going to be my friend it should be every day, or every other day if we're going to be on speaking terms at least. I understand this is going to be a somewhat high-maintenance friendship, so it's good that these fluffy little guys get a boost from wholesome pea protein powder (or if you must tinker, brown rice protein powder).

1 Blend together the pea protein powder, soy milk, water, banana, vinegar, and oil until smooth. Add both flours and the coconut sugar, baking powder, and salt. Blend until the ingredients are moistened but still slightly lumpy.

2 Oil and heat a 10- to 12-inch griddle over medium heat; it's ready for pancakes when a few drops of water flicked onto the surface sizzle. Grease the griddle each time for a new batch of pancakes.

3 Pour about ⅓ cup of batter per pancake onto the griddle, cooking only two or three at a time to leave enough room to flip. If desired, poke a few frozen (don't thaw) or fresh blueberries or walnuts onto each pancake after pouring onto the griddle. Bake for about 2 minutes, or until the edges are dry and bubbles form in the center. Flip, bake for another minute or so, and serve hot.

WHOLE-GRAIN PANCAKES

There are countless really exciting flours out there to try in pancakes. The flavor and texture will vary, as will your results. Most important, if you want to experiment, I recommend replacing only the whole wheat pastry flour with any or all of the following flours, which can be found in most natural food stores wherever fine flours are sold.

Use one or a combination of:

- White whole wheat flour (adds whole-grain goodness with a white flour taste)
- Spelt flour (slightly sweeter and moister than wheat flour)
- Rye flour (for hearty, slightly savory pancakes)
- Barley flour (lightly sweet and nutty in flavor)

Expect different flavors and textures with the addition of these flours!

SUNSHINE IN A PANCAKE

All the bright, orange-yellow flavors everybody loves in a convenient round, flat shape . . . perfect with a little syrup and vegan butter.

Add to the batter right before baking pancakes:

- ½ cup of finely grated carrot
- ½ cup of finely chopped pineapple (squeeze well to remove excess liquid)
- Grated zest of one orange (or ½ teaspoon of orange extract added to the liquid ingredients)

continued ➲

BATTER UP!

Okay, clearly I don't know sports ball. But I do know the secret ninja tricks to make a damn good pancake.

- ✘ Trick #1: Use a large mechanical ice-cream scoop to ladle the batter onto the hot griddle for perfectly round little pancakes.
- ✘ Trick #2: For easy scooping, immediately pour the blended batter into a mixing bowl. The batter thickens up considerably as its sits (that crazy protein powder!), making it tricky to scoop it out of the blender. Listen to your ninja master Terry, for she knows pancakes.

FREEZING WAFFLES AND PANCAKES

Freezing lots of waffles and pancakes will add another dimension of delicious into your weekday morning routine. You can just toss cooled waffles or pancakes in resealable plastic bags. But you maybe want a few more tips than that, such as:

✖ Pancakes may freeze better and not stick together with a small square of waxed paper or parchment paper between each one.

✦ The design of waffles makes most recipes naturally a little less sticky than pancakes, so I usually do just fine packing them without paper into bags.

✖ Frozen waffles and most pancakes do great just heated directly from the freezer in a toaster (or toaster oven). If the pancakes are rather thick or dense, thaw on a plate for a few minutes before toasting or reheating on a griddle.

BANANA COCONUT BACON CHOCOLATE CHIP PANCAKES

Inspired by the crazy-good best pancakes of the same genius combination of sweet and savory flavors served at the remarkable Seed to Sprout vegan café in Avon-by-the-Sea, New Jersey.

After pouring each pancake onto the skillet, poke into the batter the following:

- A few banana slices

- A sprinkle of vegan chocolate chips

- A scattering of *My Best Coconut Bacon* (page 18) (store-bought is swell but homemade is even better).

ALMOST OLD-FASHIONED BUCKWHEAT PANCAKES

HPP

MAKES: ABOUT 1 DOZEN (4-INCH) PANCAKES
TIME: UNDER 30 MINUTES

These buckwheat pancakes boosted with hemp protein taste like what your badass, log cabin livin', polar bear wrastlin', vegan bodybuilding grandma used to make, but are hearty AND fluffy enough for even a true protein pancake connoisseur.

1 Blend together the hemp protein powder, soy milk, water, banana, vinegar, coconut sugar, and oil until smooth. Add both flours and the baking powder, cinnamon, and salt. Blend until the dry ingredients are moistened but still slightly lumpy; don't overblend. The batter will be very thick.

2 Oil and heat a 10- to 12-inch griddle over medium heat; it's ready for pancakes when a few drops of water flicked onto the surface sizzle. Grease the griddle each time for a new batch of pancakes.

3 Pour about ⅓ cup of batter per pancake onto the griddle, cooking only two or three at a time to leave enough room to flip. Bake for about 2 minutes, or until the edges are dry and bubbles form in the center. Flip and then bake for another minute or so, until the bottoms of the pancakes are golden. Serve the pancakes hot with your choice of accompaniments.

BERRY BUCKWHEAT PANCAKES

Poke a few frozen (don't thaw) or fresh blueberries or raspberries onto each pancake after pouring onto the griddle.

⅓ cup unflavored hemp protein powder

1½ cups unsweetened plain or vanilla soy or almond milk

¼ cup water

½ cup mashed ripe banana (about 1 small banana) or unsweetened applesauce

1 tablespoon apple cider vinegar

1 tablespoon coconut sugar

1 tablespoon canola or olive oil

¾ cup buckwheat flour

⅔ cup whole wheat pastry flour

1 tablespoon baking powder

½ teaspoon ground cinnamon

½ teaspoon salt

Cooking oil spray or canola oil, for griddle

Serve with: pure maple syrup, vegan butter, fresh berries or diced fruit, toasted shelled hemp seeds, a sprinkle of cinnamon

PUMPKIN POWER PANCAKES

BRP

½ cup unflavored brown rice protein powder

1¾ cups unsweetened plain or vanilla soy or almond milk

¼ cup water

1 cup canned pure pumpkin puree

1 tablespoon apple cider vinegar

2 tablespoons melted coconut oil or olive oil

¾ cup unbleached all-purpose flour

⅔ cup whole wheat pastry flour

2 teaspoons baking powder

1½ teaspoons ground cinnamon

½ teaspoon ground ginger

½ teaspoon ground allspice

½ teaspoon salt

Cooking oil spray or canola oil, for griddle

(continued)

MAKES: ABOUT 1 DOZEN (4-INCH) PANCAKES

Pumpkin spice delights are here to stay, so it's better to just accept it. Tender pancakes loaded with pumpkin and brown rice protein powder make this a straightforward and tasty process. And if you live in a place where pumpkin-flavored everything still isn't available year-round—say, the Bizarro Universe or 2005—then this recipe should tide you over until leaf-changing season.

1 Blend together the rice protein powder, soy milk, water, pumpkin puree, vinegar, and oil until smooth. Pour into a mixing bowl, then add both flours and the baking powder, cinnamon, ginger, allspice, and salt. Pour the blended ingredients into the dry and use a rubber spatula to fold together until the dry ingredients are moistened but still slightly lumpy. The batter will be thick.

2 Oil and heat a 10- to 12-inch griddle over medium heat; it's ready for pancakes when a few drops of water flicked onto the surface sizzle. Grease the griddle each time for a new batch of pancakes.

3 Pour on about ⅓ cup of batter per pancake, cooking only two or three at a time to leave enough room to flip. Bake for about 2 minutes, or until the edges are dry and bubbles form in the center. Flip and bake for another minute or so, until the bottoms of the pancakes are golden. Serve the pancakes hot with your desired accompaniments.

SWEET POTATO OR BUTTERNUT SQUASH PANCAKES

Substitute mashed, roasted sweet potato or roasted mashed butternut squash for the pumpkin puree.

For extra zing, sprinkle some chopped walnuts onto each pancake right after pouring onto the griddle.

Additionally, try sprinkling some diced apples into the batter for a full-on fall festival in your protein pancakes.

Serve with: pure maple syrup, vegan butter, diced apples or pears, toasted chopped pecans, dried cranberries, or raisins

⅓ cup brown rice protein powder

1½ cups unsweetened plain or vanilla soy or almond milk

⅓ cup water

½ cup mashed ripe banana (about 1 small banana)

2 tablespoons canola oil or melted refined coconut oil

1 tablespoon apple cider vinegar

1 teaspoon pure vanilla or maple extract

1 cup unbleached all-purpose flour

½ cup whole wheat pastry flour

2 tablespoons organic sugar

1½ teaspoons baking powder

½ teaspoon ground cinnamon

½ teaspoon salt

Cooking oil spray or canola oil, for waffle iron

Serve with: pure maple syrup, vegan butter, fresh berries or diced fruit, toasted shelled hemp seeds, a sprinkle of cinnamon

WAKE UP WAFFLES

 BRP

MAKES: ABOUT 8 (4½-INCH) SQUARE WAFFLES
TIME: ABOUT 45 MINUTES, INCLUDING ESTIMATED BAKING TIME

These are go-to waffles for any morning that requires toasty waffles and that extra protein push. But why do I call these golden beauties Wake Up Waffles? Is it because they're great with coffee? Is it because you can't wait for nighttime to be over so you can make them? Is it because you want to bake a giant one to use as a blanket? No! (Well, all those things are true.) It's because alliteration's always awesome.

1 Blend together the rice protein powder, soy milk, water, banana, oil, vinegar, and vanilla until smooth. In a mixing bowl, combine the flours, sugar, baking powder, cinnamon, and salt. Pour the blended ingredients into the dry and use a rubber spatula to fold together until the dry ingredients are moistened but still slightly lumpy.

2 Preheat your waffle iron according to the manufacturer's directions. Lightly oil both griddles of the iron before adding the batter.

3 Pour in about ⅓ cup of batter per waffle for square waffles or ½ cup of batter for larger Belgian-style round waffles. Bake until the waffle iron almost stops steaming, or according to the manufacturer's directions.

4 Serve hot with all the proper waffle fixin's. Waffles freeze beautifully, too: Seal in resealable plastic bags and freeze for up to 2 months. Reheat in a toaster or toaster oven.

GOLDEN CORN HEMP PROTEIN WAFFLES

HPP

MAKES: ABOUT 10 (4½-INCH) SQUARE WAFFLES
TIME: ABOUT 45 MINUTES, INCLUDING ESTIMATED BAKING TIME

⅓ cup unflavored hemp protein powder

1½ cups unsweetened plain or vanilla soy or almond milk

⅓ cup water

½ cup mashed ripe banana (about 1 small banana)

1 tablespoon apple cider vinegar

3 tablespoons organic sugar

2 tablespoons melted coconut oil or olive oil

1 cup yellow cornmeal

⅔ cup whole wheat pastry flour

1½ teaspoons baking powder

½ teaspoon salt

Cooking oil spray or canola oil, for waffle iron

Serve with: pure maple syrup, vegan butter, fresh berries or diced fruit, toasted shelled hemp seeds, toasted pecans

Waffles are the ninjas of breakfast fare: all those little squares are like sneaky pockets. Instead of shuriken and smoke bombs, waffles conceal a pat of vegan butter, some fresh berries, or dollops of syrup . . . and for protein ninjas like us, these gridiron gut-busters hide a good amount of hemp protein powder. Cornmeal also arms this batter for waffles with a not-too-sweet, crunchy golden corn bread texture.

1 Blend together the hemp protein powder, soy milk, water, banana, vinegar, sugar, and oil until smooth. In a mixing bowl, combine the cornmeal, flour, baking powder, and salt. Pour the blended ingredients into the dry and use a rubber spatula to fold together until the dry ingredients are just moistened but still slightly lumpy. The batter will be very thick.

2 Preheat your waffle iron according to the manufacturer's directions. Lightly oil the waffle iron; depending on your iron, you may need to do this for every waffle batch, or perhaps only the first one or two as the iron continues to heat up.

3 Pour in about ½ cup of batter per waffle or more, depending on the size of your waffle iron. Bake until the waffle iron almost stops steaming, or according to the manufacturer's directions.

4 Serve hot with all the fixin's, even your favorite vegan ice cream (at breakfast? I don't judge).

LEMON POPPY SEED CORN WAFFLES

Grate the zest from one organic lemon and add to the soy milk.

Replace the apple cider vinegar with the juice of one lemon.

Whisk 2 tablespoons of poppy seeds into the dry ingredients before adding the wet ingredients.

WAFFLES ALL THE TIME!

Waffles were practically made for freezing and reheat perfectly in toasters and toaster ovens. That's why supermarket freezer cases are stocked floor to shelf with frozen waffles of all varieties.

Instead of relying on the waffle industrial complex for your instant frozen waffle needs, make a double batch of batter anytime you get a hankering for waffles. Let the extra waffles cool completely, then pack tightly in doubled resealable plastic bags. Freeze and consume within 2 months!

PEANUT BUTTER & RASPBERRY FRENCH TOAST SANDWICHES

PPP LP NSP

SERVES: 4
TIME: 30 MINUTES

FRENCH TOAST PROTEIN BATTER

2 tablespoons garbanzo bean flour

2 tablespoons pea protein powder

2 tablespoons cashew pieces

¾ cup sweetened vanilla almond or soy milk

Pinch of salt

Dash of vanilla extract

SANDWICH FILLING

¼ cup smooth natural peanut butter

1 large ripe banana

1 tablespoon pure maple syrup

½ teaspoon ground cinnamon

Yes, you read that right: peanut butter raspberry French toast sandwiches. Say it out loud. Yell it from the rooftops. (WAIT, ninjas don't yell.) Fresh fruit, nut butter, protein powder, and a protein-loaded batter: a magnificent protein loaded Frankenbreakfast for the protein ninja who cannot and will not compromise! Bonus: This uses up day-old bread. Ninjas do not waste.

If raspberries aren't your thing, strawberries will do.

1 Blend together the French toast batter ingredients until smooth and pour into a shallow baking dish.

2 Make the sandwich filling: Mash together the peanut butter, banana, maple syrup, and cinnamon into a chunky paste.

3 Assemble the sandwich fingers: Divide the filling evenly among the four slices of bread and spread all the way to the edges. Divide the raspberries between two of the slices, mashing them in an even layer all the way to the edges. Top each with the two remaining slices of bread and press down on each sandwich to squish slightly. Slice each sandwich in half, either into rectangles or triangles.

4 Spread the sandwiches in the batter-filled baking dish. Set aside to soak for 10 minutes, occasionally flipping over your fingers, until most of the batter has been absorbed.

5 Lightly oil a well-seasoned cast-iron skillet and heat over medium heat. Spread another thin layer of oil on the hot pan and add half of the fingers. Fry on each side for 4 to 5 minutes, gently pressing down with the back of a spatula occasionally. Repeat with the remaining sandwich fingers. Serve hot with sliced fresh fruit or berries and maple syrup.

AVOCADO & COCONUT BACON FRENCH TOAST

You're sweet enough, so here's a savory version.

Omit the sugar and vanilla extract from the batter.

Fill the sandwiches with a smear of the spread from *White Bean & Cashew Ricotta Toast* (page 111) or your favorite hummus. Top with very thin slices of avocado and a generous sprinkle of *My Best Coconut Bacon* (page 18). Remember to get the filling all the way to the very edge!

SANDWICH FINGERS

½ cup thawed, drained raspberries or fresh raspberries

4 slices whole wheat bread, a few days old (very fresh bread will fall apart)

Vegetable oil, for frying

Serve with: sliced fresh fruit or berries and pure maple syrup

PANCAKES, WAFFLES + MORE

TEMPEH BACON STRIPS

SP

SERVES: 3 OR 4
TIME: LESS THAN 30 MINUTES

It's impossible to have a chapter about vegan breakfast foods, let alone protein-intense breakfast foods, without offering a no-nonsense, always tasty recipe for tempeh bacon. Sure, you could buy a package of bacon-flavored tempeh to speed along the process. I often do myself. But sometimes the homemade stuff—smoky, sweet, salty— is even easier than a trip to the store.

1 Slice the tempeh into ¼-inch-thick strips. It's easiest to slice the strips from the narrowest side first, for shorter, easier-to-fry pieces. Or slice the strips lengthwise instead, for properly bacon-length strips. Either way, it's gonna be tasty.

2 In a ceramic or metal baking dish, whisk together the remaining ingredients until smooth. Layer the tempeh strips in the marinade and soak for 4 minutes. Gently turn the strips over and press into the remaining marinade. Let stand for another 3 to 4 minutes. Or cover the dish and chill overnight.

3 Heat a lightly oiled cast-iron skillet over medium heat. Lay in the tempeh pieces in a single layer. Don't crowd the pan; fry in two or three batches for best results. Cook until well browned on one side, then flip and cook the other side until browned, 2 to 3 minutes per side. If the tempeh looks dry, drizzle with a little extra oil before flipping. Serve hot with pancakes, waffles, or biscuits!

1 (8-ounce block) tempeh

2 tablespoons pure maple syrup

2 tablespoons tamari

2 tablespoons all-natural ketchup

1 tablespoon olive or canola oil, plus more for skillet

½ teaspoon smoked sweet paprika

½ teaspoon hickory or mesquite liquid smoke

PANCAKES, WAFFLES + MORE

TEMPEH SAUSAGE SAGE GRAVY

2 tablespoons extra-virgin olive oil

4 ounces tempeh, crumbled (1 cup crumbled)

2 teaspoons fennel seeds

2 garlic cloves, peeled and minced

2 teaspoons tamari, plus more to taste (optional)

1 cup diced yellow onion

3 tablespoons unbleached all-purpose or garbanzo bean flour

2 cups vegan vegetable broth

½ teaspoon dried thyme

½ teaspoon rubbed dried sage

Freshly ground black pepper

MAKES: ABOUT 3 CUPS GRAVY
TIME: 30 MINUTES

If you are missing sausagy goodness, you, my friend, are in luck. Gently browned tempeh and fennel seeds add that special kick to this creamy, stick-to-your-ribs breakfast gravy. Pour it on everything or simply bathe in it.

1 Heat 1 tablespoon of the olive oil in a large saucepan over medium heat. Add the tempeh, fennel seeds, and garlic and sauté for 5 minutes, until the tempeh is golden. Sprinkle with the tamari, transfer from the pan to a bowl, and set aside.

2 Lower the heat to low and heat the remaining 1 tablespoon of the olive oil, add the onion, and fry for 2 minutes to soften up the onion. Stir in the flour and cook for 2 minutes.

3 Stir in the broth, thyme, and sage. Use an immersion blender to pulse the mixture to a desired consistency in the pan; either leave it a little bit chunky or blend until silky smooth. Stir in the fried tempeh and cook, stirring occasionally, for 5 minutes, until the gravy is thickened and hot. Season with black pepper to taste and a dash or two of more tamari, if desired. Remove from the heat and serve hot with freshly baked biscuits, waffles, or a simple salad and *Edamame Spelt Flatbread* (page 83).

PRO-TIP: *Any veggie gravy is only as good as the vegetable broth in it, so make sure to use a flavorful one, such as Better Than Bouillon or a great homemade broth.*

BUTTON UP WHITE BEAN GRAVY

LP

MAKES: ABOUT 2½ CUPS GRAVY
TIME: ABOUT 40 MINUTES

Ahh, gravy. Few things in life can look like lumpy gray sludge and still make us drool. One is Harrison Ford. The other is bean gravy. A necessary breakfast and brunch staple, mop it up with *Fluffy Rice Protein Drop Biscuits* (page 75) or *Sweet Potato Pea Biscuits* (page 79), or even serve on any hearty burger in this book.

1 Heat the oil in a large saucepan over medium heat. Add the onion and garlic and cook for 3 minutes, stirring frequently, or until the onion is translucent. Stir in the mushrooms, sprinkle with the tamari, and cook for 5 minutes, stirring frequently, or until the mushrooms are tender but still juicy.

2 Decrease the heat to low and stir in the flour. Cook, stirring constantly, for 2 minutes, or until the mixture turns slightly beige, is bubbly, and appears to have grown in volume.

continued

> **PRO-TIP**: *Pluck the leaves off the stem of fresh thyme, this time or anytime when it's time for thyme.*

2 tablespoons extra-virgin olive oil

1 cup diced yellow onion

3 garlic cloves, peeled and chopped

6 ounces white button mushrooms, roughly chopped (2 cups)

1 tablespoon tamari

2 tablespoons unbleached all-purpose or garbanzo bean flour

1 (16-ounce) can navy beans, drained and rinsed

1½ cups vegan vegetable broth

1 teaspoon dried thyme, or 1 tablespoon fresh

Freshly ground black pepper

Salt (optional)

PANCAKES, WAFFLES + MORE

NOTE

The gravy can be made up to 2 days in advance and refrigerated, tightly covered. Reheat it over low heat, stirring occasionally.

3 Increase the heat to medium, and slowly whisk in the beans, broth, and thyme. Bring the mixture to a boil, lower the heat to low, and simmer the sauce for 5 minutes, or until it thickens. Use an immersion blender to chop the mixture to a desired consistency in the pan: Either leave it a little bit chunky or blend until silky smooth. This can also be done in a food processor fitted with the steel blade or in a blender.

4 Season to taste with black pepper and salt, if desired. Remove the gravy from the heat and serve hot with freshly baked biscuits, toast, or your favorite aging childhood *Star Wars* heartthrob.

PRO-TIP: *If you've made your way through the Tempeh Sausage Gravy recipe, this will be old news. If not: Any veggie gravy is only as good as the vegetable broth in it, so make sure to use a flavorful one, such as Better Than Bouillon or a great homemade broth.*

MAPLE BREAKFAST SAUSAGES

MAKES: 16 SMALL SAUSAGES
TIME: 45 MINUTES

As if breathable air wasn't enough, trees also gift us with maple syrup. Thank you, trees! That touch of sweetness elevates these savory little wieners into a mighty satisfying breakfast. Serve with any of the pancakes in this book or the *Baked Veggie Pan Omelet* (page 70). They also freeze well if you want to make a double batch —they're one of my go-to add-ins for stir-fries, especially the refried quinoa in *Black Bean Hemp Burger Bowl with Refried Corn Quinoa and Mango Chia Salsa* (page 160).

1 Preheat the oven to 400°F. Tear eight pieces of foil, each about 6 inches wide.

2 In a mixing bowl, mash the beans with a fork into a creamy paste. Stir in the vegetable broth, tamari, maple syrup, and canola oil.

3 In a separate bowl, combine all the dry ingredients, except the whole wheat flour, forming a well in the center. Pour the wet ingredients into the well, stirring with a fork until all the liquid has been absorbed. Now, roll up your sleeves and use your hands to knead the mixture in the bowl for 1½ to 2 minutes, or until smooth.

continued ⟳

½ cup cooked navy beans, drained and rinsed

⅔ cup vegan vegetable broth

3 tablespoons tamari

3 tablespoons pure maple syrup

1 tablespoon canola oil

1 cup vital wheat gluten flour

¼ cup unflavored pea protein powder

¼ cup garbanzo bean flour

1 teaspoon rubbed sage powder

½ teaspoon dried thyme

½ teaspoon garlic powder

½ teaspoon smoked sweet paprika

¼ teaspoon freshly ground black pepper

A little bit of whole wheat flour

Olive oil, for sautéing (optional)

4 Transfer the mixture to a lightly floured cutting board and shape into a log about 2 inches thick. Slice into sixteen pieces by cutting the log into four pieces, and then each piece into four slices. Shape each slice into small sausage shapes and wrap each individually like a piece of candy in aluminum foil, twisting the ends together. Don't wrap each piece too tightly; give it a little slack, as the mixture will expand as it steams during the baking process. Bake on an oven sheet for 20 minutes, flipping each sausage over once about halfway into the baking time.

5 Serve hot, or for a properly browned exterior, lightly sauté the sausages in a little olive oil in a cast-iron pan over medium-high heat until browned on the edges.

TEMPEH APPLE SAGE SAUSAGE PATTIES

MAKES: 10 LARGE PATTIES
TIME: ABOUT 30 MINUTES

1 (8-ounce) package tempeh

1 cup cooked red kidney beans, drained and rinsed

1 cup finely cored, chopped, unpeeled green apple (about 1 small apple)

3 tablespoons tamari

1 tablespoon olive oil, plus more for frying

2 garlic cloves, peeled and minced

2 teaspoons fennel seeds

2 teaspoons sweet paprika

½ teaspoon dried sage

¼ teaspoon salt, or more to taste

¼ cup garbanzo bean flour, for coating

This is a crowd-pleasing breakfast snack, assuming you have crowds over for breakfast (I want to go to your parties). The mashed up tempeh adds firm and hearty texture, satisfying all. The patties freeze nicely, and I recommend tucking leftover ones into *Fluffy Rice Protein Drop Biscuits* (page 75). And—why not—drench them in *Button Up White Bean Gravy* (page 59). Do it, I say!

1 Dice the tempeh into 1-inch cubes. In a small saucepan, cover the tempeh with 2 inches of cold water and bring to a boil. Lower the heat to low, partially cover, and simmer the tempeh for 5 minutes, or until soft. Drain and transfer to a large mixing bowl.

2 Add the remaining ingredients, except the garbanzo flour. Thoroughly mash everything to form a thick, chunky mixture. Taste and season with more salt, if desired. Divide the mixture into ten equal-size balls, and roll each ball in garbanzo bean flour. Gently pat each ball into a patty about ½ inch thick.

3 Slick the bottom of a cast-iron skillet with olive oil and heat over medium heat. Fry half of the patties at a time, heating more olive oil in the pan with each batch as needed to prevent sticking. Carefully flip each after 3 to 4 minutes per side, or until both sides are golden brown. Serve hot or at room temperature.

GARBANZO VEGGIE PANCAKES WITH CILANTRO MINT APPLE CHUTNEY

GF   LP   BRP

MAKES: ABOUT 8 (4-INCH) PANCAKES
TIME: ABOUT 1 HOUR

These robust, supersavory garbanzo flour and brown rice pancakes are inspired by *pudla*, a type of Indian breakfast crepe. These are a little heftier than classic *pudla* and a little richer with the addition of coconut milk, but if you're training for a big ninja fight and need to fit into your tightest yellow jumpsuit, substitute water or plain coconut water for the coconut milk. While you can make them very plain with only pantry staples, mixing in fresh grated or chopped veggies makes them memorable and a complete meal that will keep you going all through the day. And don't forget the fresh cilantro mint chutney!

1 In a blender, pulse all of the ingredients, except the cooking oil spray, until smooth. Cover and refrigerate for 10 minutes. Ideally the batter should be chilled for an hour or overnight.

2 Heat a well-seasoned cast-iron or steel pan over medium-high heat. Generously spray the pan with cooking oil, or for richer-tasting pancakes, brush with melted coconut oil. The griddle is ready to use when water flicked onto the surface sizzles immediately.

continued ➲

1½ cups garbanzo bean flour

½ cup brown rice protein powder

½ cup full-fat coconut milk

1 cup water

½ teaspoon ground turmeric

½ teaspoon ground cumin

½ teaspoon ground ginger, or 1 teaspoon grated fresh

½ teaspoon cayenne pepper

1 teaspoon salt

Cooking oil spray or melted refined coconut oil, for frying

PANCAKES, WAFFLES + MORE

3 If adding veggies (see the variations that follow), stir them into the batter before cooking. Ladle ⅓ cup of batter onto the griddle, starting in a spiral in the center and working outward. Fry for 3 minutes, or until the top is dry and the edges are browned, spray the top with more cooking oil spray, then loosen with a spatula and carefully flip over. Fry for another 2 minutes, then transfer to a plate.

4 Fold and eat! Serve hot with fresh *Cilantro Mint Apple Chutney*.

ENDLESS VARIATIONS

This savory chickpea batter is so easy to play with! Go for a traditional Indian vibe and fold these into the batter:

- ½ cup of roughly chopped fresh cilantro
- 1 to 2 teaspoons of grated fresh ginger in place of the ground ginger
- 1 to 2 teaspoons of grated fresh turmeric in place of the ground turmeric
- One to two small fresh red or green chile peppers in place of the cayenne pepper
- 1 teaspoon of nigella (black cumin) seeds
- 1 teaspoon of cumin or fennel seeds

Then add fresh veggies, such as:

- ½ cup of thinly sliced red or white onion
- ½ cup of finely chopped scallions
- 1 cup of finely chopped spinach or arugula
- One grated carrot
- 1 cup of firmly packed grated summer squash

Cilantro Mint Apple Chutney

A fresh light chutney that is best made in small batches and eaten immediately.

1 Blend together the coconut, cilantro, mint, water, lemon juice, and salt until almost smooth. It's best to leave a little texture. Pour into a mixing bowl, stir in the grated apple, and serve immediately.

½ cup dried shredded unsweetened coconut

1 cup firmly packed fresh cilantro leaves

½ cup firmly packed fresh mint leaves

¼ cup water

2 tablespoons freshly squeezed lemon juice

½ teaspoon salt

1 large tart apple, cored and grated (don't peel)

EARLY BIRD SCRAMBLED TOFU

SP   LP

SERVES: 2–3

TIME: ABOUT 40 MINUTES, NOT INCLUDING MARINATING TIME

There are so many tofu scrambles in the world! I lay no claim as master of any: You should remain suspicious of anyone that does, after all. After years of eating the stuff in many forms, I have a fondness for the unusual nutritional-yeast drenched version toted by Bouldin Creek Cafe in Austin, Texas. You'll feel like a fifteenth-level vegan, pouring on the yeast to finish off this cheery golden dish. Yes, this recipe is even more protein warrior worthy with gently mashed chickpeas and then amped with the most umami-loaded of ingredients (miso and mushrooms). Why do you just stand there and stare at me like that? Just give in to this ultrahearty eggless scramble.

1 (14-ounce) can chickpeas, drained and rinsed

1 pound extra-firm tofu, undrained

1 cup sliced button or shiitake mushrooms

1 large yellow onion, peeled and diced

2 garlic cloves, peeled and chopped

1 heaping rounded tablespoon white or yellow miso

2 teaspoons mustard powder

1 teaspoon ground turmeric

1 teaspoon salt

½ teaspoon ground cumin

½ teaspoon ground sweet paprika

½ teaspoon freshly ground black pepper

2 tablespoons vegetable oil, for frying

2 cups baby spinach

½ cup nutritional yeast

1 Slightly crush the chickpeas with a potato masher or fork in a large mixing bowl. Crumble in the tofu. Add all the remaining ingredients, except the vegetable oil, spinach, and nutritional yeast. Stir everything together (hands are particularly good at this) until the miso is dissolved. Cover and chill for an hour or overnight.

2 When it's scramble time, heat the vegetable oil in a large, deep skillet over medium heat. Add the marinated tofu and fry for 6 to 8 minutes, stirring occasionally with a wooden spoon or heat-resistant silicone spatula. Fold in the spinach and fry for another 2 to 3 minutes, or until the spinach is wilted and most of the liquid from the tofu has been absorbed.

3 Just as the tofu looks firm and is starting to brown, sprinkle on the nutritional yeast. Fold in the yeast for about 30 seconds, just long enough to coat the tofu but before it completely melts. Serve the tofu hot with toast or the Harissa Roasted Sweet Potatoes from *Sunny Oat Burger Bowl* (page 151).

PRO-TIP: *Most recipes ask you to drain and press the tofu, only to add more water at the end. The controversial method of just leaving the tofu unmolested and letting it mellow in the fridge yields a tender, flavorful tofu.*

BAKED VEGGIE PAN OMELET

MAKES: ONE 11 X 7 X 2-INCH OMELET, SERVING 4-6
TIME: 1 HOUR

ROASTED VEGGIES

2 tablespoons extra-virgin olive oil, plus more to regrease pan

1 large leek, trimmed and sliced on an angle into 1-inch pieces

2 large carrots, peeled and sliced lengthwise

1 large red onion, peeled and sliced into thick half-moons

1 cup green beans, ends trimmed

1 pint cherry tomatoes, sliced in half

2 tablespoons fresh rosemary or thyme, or 1 tablespoon dried

Salt and freshly ground black pepper

(continued)

The protein ninja and the veggie ninja (did you miss that book? It's a sneaky one!) teamed up for this one. You can sneak many veggies in this dish and make your mom happy. In this base recipe, I went with summery flavors (plus I like telling people to take one large leek), but root vegetables and tubers make this a heftier dish in the colder months. Like a frittata or Spanish tortilla, this baked omelet tastes as good cold as it does hot. You can even stick it between some bread for a sandwich. That's right, I told you where to stick it. Ninja don't care.

1 Prepare the veggies: Preheat the oven to 350°F. Toss together the olive oil, leek, carrots, onion, green beans, tomatoes, and herbs in a 9 x 13 x 2-inch baking dish. When everything is coated with oil, spread in an even layer in the pan. Sprinkle a little salt and pepper on top.

2 Roast the veggies for about 30 minutes, stirring occasionally, until golden and tender. Remove the pan from the oven and transfer the vegetables to a dish or cutting board. When the baking pan is just cool enough to touch, line with foil (maybe slip on a pair of baking mitts for this part). Generously grease the foil with additional olive oil.

3 Make the omelet: In a blender, pulse together until smooth the tofu, soy milk, garbanzo bean flour, nutritional yeast, olive oil, mustard, baking powder, turmeric, salt, and *kala namak*, if using. Pour into the pan and gently shake the pan a few times to remove any air bubbles.

continued

OMELET

16 ounces soft silken tofu

½ cup unsweetened plain soy milk

⅔ cup garbanzo bean flour

3 tablespoons nutritional yeast

2 heaping tablespoons whole-grain mustard

1 tablespoon olive oil

½ teaspoon baking powder

½ teaspoon ground turmeric

1 teaspoon salt

Generous pinch of *kala namak* (Indian black salt) (optional)

NOTE

If you cannot locate any kala namak (Indian black salt) or just don't want to use it in this recipe, just leave it out entirely.

4 Arrange the roasted vegetables on top of the tofu mixture in a pleasing way. Return the pan to the oven and bake for 20 to 25 minutes, or until the tofu layer is lightly puffed, golden, and no longer liquid but instead a soft, solid texture when poked with a knife.

5 Remove from the oven and set aside to cool for at least 5 minutes before slicing. Use a spatula to gently remove squares of the omelet from the pan. The tofu will firm up considerably if chilled overnight and reheats well.

THE PROTEIN BAKERY BASKET

This chapter is where it all started. This is the scone-shaped heart of the protein ninja.

After over a year of salads writing *Salad Samurai*, though wonderful and healthy, I just wanted to bake again. I love the process, the chemistry, and the artistry, and most of all, the supertasty results of mixing pulverized grains and fats and other goodies together and blasting them with heat.

However, after even more years of cupcakes and pies and cookies, I knew I was to return to my roots: wholesome baked goods. Sort of. I still use some unbleached all-purpose flour and organic sugar occasionally to lighten things up, but my style is rustic, full of whole grains, nuts, and dried fruits. And I don't "decorate." These are simple, good-enough-for-you, everyday baked goods. With one exception . . .

. . . the addition of plant-based protein! The ease and intriguing textures and flavors of unflavored, unsweetened hemp, brown rice, and pea protein made their way into my muffins, cookies, and scones. There's only so many things I can eat in one day, and yeah, why not make that scone slightly smarter than the average baked good?

You'll see that I still like variety when it comes to ingredients. For example, a modest amount of organic cane sugar goes into baked goods for those new to vegan protein baking. But I adore using coconut sugar and maple syrup in my superwholesome recipes—no-cane-sugar-means-healthy fans, take note.

How do I make the most of these protein-loaded treats? Pick a day or weeknight evening and bake two or three recipes, let cool completely, seal tightly in resealable plastic bags, and freeze. Busy mornings or even snacks with a healthy edge are as easy as tossing one of these in your commuter bag before work or leaving it on the counter to thaw for ten minutes!

ALMOST FROZEN OIL!

Some of these recipes call for almost frozen oil. If you've never tossed your EVOO or coconut oils into the deep freeze, ninja is here to tell you how to nearly freeze oil: Pour the oil into a small plastic container, then pop into the freezer for 20 to 25 minutes, or until very thick and cloudy. The oil should have the consistency of a sorbet. If too frozen, just leave on the counter for about 5 minutes until softened.

FLUFFY RICE PROTEIN DROP BISCUITS

BRP

MAKES: 8 LARGE BISCUITS
TIME: ABOUT 45 MINUTES

These biscuits (fluffy, drop) have that buttermilk quality (nondairy milk + apple cider vinegar = buttermilk curdle). Easy-peasy (or easy brown-ricey), double—or triple—the batch and freeze 'em for grab-and-go. These are great with *Tempeh Bacon Strips* (page 55), *Tempeh Sausage Sage Gravy* (page 56), *Button Up White Bean Gravy* (page 59), or *Tempeh Apple Sage Sausage Patties* (page 64). This biscuit is essentially an empty (but not empty-caloried) canvas upon which you can make your masterpiece. Or simply eat the canvas. That's what I do, and that's why I'm no longer allowed back to the Louvre.

1 Preheat the oven to 425°F and line a baking sheet with parchment paper.

2 Whisk together the soy milk and vinegar in a liquid measuring cup and set aside to curdle for 5 minutes. Meanwhile, in a large mixing bowl, stir together the flour, rice protein powder, baking powder, and salt.

3 Scoop the almost frozen oil into the flour, then use a fork or a pastry cutter to cut the fat into the flour to create a crumbly mixture. If the oil starts to get too melty, set the bowl in the freezer for a few minutes to keep everything cold. Form a well in the center of the flour mixture.

4 Pour in the curdled soy milk, then stir only enough to moisten the dry ingredients and form a soft dough. Lightly rub your hands with a little oil, then divide the dough into eight equal pieces. Shape into balls, oiling your

1¼ cups unsweetened soy or other nondairy milk

1 tablespoon apple cider vinegar

1¾ cups unbleached all-purpose flour, plus more for dusting

½ cup brown rice protein powder

1 tablespoon baking powder

1 teaspoon salt

¼ cup refined coconut oil or canola oil, almost frozen (see sidebar, page 73), or cold vegan margarine

Additional vegetable oil, for forming

continued

hands as necessary, and transfer to the prepared baking sheet, leaving about 2 inches apart, and flatten slightly. Bake for 20 to 24 minutes, or until the bottom of the biscuits are golden brown. Serve hot, or when cool, split in half and toast on a griddle.

COCONUT BACON SPINACH BISCUITS

Along with the wet ingredients, add 1 cup of finely chopped, cooked spinach and ½ cup of coconut bacon, either homemade (page 18) or purchased. Press a few slivers of coconut bacon on top of each scone.

STOP THE DROP AND ROLL

Unlike what the name suggests, instead of making lazy, I mean uniquely shaped, drop biscuits, you most certainly may cut the dough with a biscuit cutter for cute, perfectly round pucks.

First, before mixing the dough, generously flour a work surface. Have handy a little extra flour and a 2½- to 3-inch round cookie or biscuit cutter.

After adding the liquid ingredients to the dry, stir only enough to moisten the dough and gather it into a ball. Drop the dough onto the surface and dust the top generously with flour. By hand, pat the dough into a circle about an inch thick.

Cut the dough into biscuits, dipping the cutter into flour whenever it starts to stick to the dough. Gather up the remaining scraps once and divide and shape into biscuits. And here's the amazing tip Carla Hall (yes, that Carla Hall of *Top Chef!*) gave me for ideal biscuits: Flip them over and put them upside down on the baking sheet. Such pretty round biscuits that look great out of the oven.

Last tip: Make sure the oven is properly preheated and very hot. If your biscuits are coming out a bit pale, bake the biscuits at a slightly higher temperature, about 25°F hotter.

HEMPY CORN BREAD

HPP

MAKES: 1 (8-INCH) SQUARE OR 1 (10-INCH) CAST-IRON SKILLET CORN BREAD
TIME: 50 MINUTES

Corn bread: that hearty, grainy, slightly sweet base for vegan butter or mop for beans, gravy, and other sorts of deliciousness. Here the addition of hemp ups both the protein and the hearty/crunchy ante, while adding a bit of a nutty flavor. (What, did you think I'd name this Corny Corn Bread?)

1 Preheat the oven to 350°F, and place a 10-inch cast-iron skillet in the oven as it preheats.

2 Combine the soy milk, hemp protein powder, canola oil, sugar, and vinegar in a blender or food processor fitted with the steel blade. Pulse until smooth. Combine the cornmeal, white whole wheat flour, baking powder, baking soda, and salt in a large mixing bowl, and whisk well.

3 Form a well in the center of the dry ingredients and pour in the soy milk mixture. Stir just enough to moisten the dry ingredients. Remove the skillet from the oven, and generously wipe the interior with a paper towel dipped in coconut oil. Scrape the batter into the skillet, leveling the top with a rubber spatula. Sprinkle the hemp seeds on top.

continued ➲

2 cups plain soy or almond milk

½ cup hemp protein powder

¼ cup canola oil

¼ cup coconut sugar

1 tablespoon apple cider vinegar

1¾ cups cornmeal or corn flour

½ cup white whole wheat or unbleached all-purpose flour

1 tablespoon baking powder

1 teaspoon baking soda

½ teaspoon salt

Coconut oil, for pan

2 tablespoons hemp seeds, for garnish

PROTEIN BAKERY BASKET

NOTE

The batter can also be baked in an 8-inch square pan. Line the bottom of the pan with parchment paper and then spray the bottom and sides lightly with cooking oil spray. Bake the bread for 35 to 38 minutes. It will not have the same browned and crisp crust as one baked in a skillet.

4 Bake the bread in the center of the oven for 25 to 30 minutes, or until a toothpick inserted into the center comes out clean. Remove the skillet from the oven and let the pan cool on a wire rack for 5 minutes before serving. Store leftover corn bread refrigerated in an airtight container.

PRO-TIP: *When it comes to corn bread, I've been won over by the light and smooth style that can only happen by using corn flour. Made popular by the surge in gluten-free baking, you can find a great one made by Bob's Red Mill in most supermarkets that stock gluten-free baking ingredients. Or just order it online along with your toilet paper and garbage bags, like everybody else.*

SWEET POTATO PEA BISCUITS

PPP

MAKES: 12 LARGE BISCUITS

TIME: ABOUT 45 MINUTES, NOT INCLUDING ROASTING SWEET POTATOES

Roasted mashed sweet potato adds that right amount of moisture along with appealing sweetness, golden color, and flavor to these tender baking powder biscuits boosted with pea protein. Treat 'em as you would any other biscuit: with sausage, bacon, gravy, Tater Tots, whatever your secret ninja heart desires.

1 Preheat the oven to 350°F and line a baking sheet with parchment paper.

2 In a blender, pulse together the soy milk, sweet potato, and vinegar until smooth. Meanwhile, in a large mixing bowl, stir together the flour, pea protein powder, baking powder, baking soda, and salt.

3 Scoop the almost frozen oil into the flour mixture, then use a fork or a pastry cutter to cut the fat into the flour until the mixture is crumbly. Form a well in the center of the flour.

4 Pour in the soy milk mixture, then stir only enough to moisten the dry ingredients and form a soft, somewhat sticky dough. Generously flour a work surface, turn out the dough onto the surface, and dust the top generously with flour. By hand, pat the dough into a circle about an inch thick.

continued ➔

1 cup unsweetened soy or other nondairy milk

1 cup mashed roasted sweet potato

1 tablespoon apple cider vinegar

2¼ cups unbleached all-purpose flour, plus more for dusting

½ cup pea protein powder

1 tablespoon baking powder

1 teaspoon baking soda

1 teaspoon salt

¼ cup refined coconut oil or canola oil, almost frozen (see sidebar, page 73) or cold vegan margarine

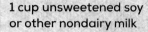

PROTEIN BAKERY BASKET

5 Dust a 2- to 3-inch biscuit cutter with flour. Cut the dough into biscuits, dipping the cutter into flour whenever it starts to stick to the dough. Gather up the remaining scraps once and divide and shape into biscuits. Transfer to the prepared baking sheet and bake for 20 to 24 minutes, or until the bottoms of the biscuits are light golden brown; do not overbake. Serve hot, or when cool, split in half and toast on a griddle.

PRO-TIP: *To prepare the sweet potato, don't peel or pierce, just place the whole unpeeled sweet potato on a rimmed baking sheet and roast at 400°F for 30 to 35 minutes, or until very soft and easily pierced with a fork. Slice in half to speed up the cooling.*

OLIVE ROSEMARY BISCUITS

MAKES: 8 LARGE BISCUITS
TIME: ABOUT 45 MINUTES

Just when you thought you'd already gone to biscuit heaven, here's another divinely flavored, protein-laden vehicle for sausage or any other fixin's. Too angelic? Check out the seitan version that follows.

1 Preheat the oven to 425°F and line a baking sheet with parchment paper.

2 Whisk together the soy milk and lemon juice in a liquid measuring cup and set aside to curdle for 5 minutes. Meanwhile, in a large mixing bowl, stir together the flour, rice protein powder, baking powder, and salt.

3 Scoop the almost frozen oil into the flour, then use a fork or a pastry cutter to cut the fat into the flour to create a crumbly mixture. If the oil starts to get too melty, set the bowl in the freezer for a few minutes to keep everything cold. Form a well in the center of the flour mixture.

4 Pour in the curdled soy milk, olives, and rosemary. Stir only enough to moisten the dry ingredients; the dough will be soft. Lightly rub your hands with a little oil, then divide the dough into eight equal pieces. Shape into balls, oiling your hands as necessary, transfer to the prepared baking sheet, leaving about 2 inches apart, and flatten slightly. Bake for 20 to 24 minutes, or until the bottoms of the biscuits are golden brown. Serve hot, or when, cool split in half and toast on a griddle.

continued ➲

1¼ cups unsweetened soy or other nondairy milk

1 tablespoon freshly squeezed lemon juice

1¾ cups unbleached all-purpose flour

½ cup brown rice protein powder

1 tablespoon baking powder

½ teaspoon salt

¼ cup extra-virgin olive oil, almost frozen (see sidebar, page 73)

1 cup roughly chopped oil-cured black olives

1 tablespoon dried rosemary, or 3 tablespoons fresh, roughly chopped

Additional olive oil, for forming

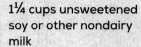

PROTEIN BAKERY BASKET

SPICY SEITAN BISCUITS

You read it right: These hearty biscuits are going to hell in a bread basket.

Omit the olives and the rosemary.

Before you add the wet stuff, stir into the flour mixture 1 tablespoon of smoked hot paprika and ½ teaspoon of cayenne pepper. Then, in place of where you'd add the olives, add 1 cup of finely chopped seitan and two finely chopped scallions. Sprinkle the tops of each biscuit with a little smoked paprika before baking.

EDAMAME SPELT FLATBREADS

SP

MAKES: 8 LARGE FLATBREADS
TIME: ABOUT 45 MINUTES

Maybe it's the tortilla lover in me: these fast-cooking, charmingly green flatbreads (thanks pureed edamame!) are great with curries, the gravies in the breakfast chapter, or as an alternative foundation for the savory toast toppings.

1 In a blender, blend together the edamame and water until as smooth as possible.

2 In a mixing bowl, combine the spelt flour and salt. Add the coconut oil and use your fingers to rub the oil into the flour to form sandy crumbs. Form a well in the center, then add the edamame mixture and the chopped scallions. Stir to form a soft dough.

3 Turn out the dough onto a floured surface and knead for a minute. Divide the dough into eight equal pieces, roll into balls, cover with a damp, clean kitchen towel, and set aside to rest for 10 minutes.

4 Preheat a cast-iron griddle over medium-high heat. With a lightly floured rolling pin, roll each piece of dough into a circle about ¼ inch thick. Have ready a large, clean kitchen towel.

5 Cook each flatbread on the hot skillet for 3 to 4 minutes per side, or until toasted and browned in spots. Stack the cooked breads on top of each other, nested in the kitchen towel. Fold the towel over the breads to keep them soft and warm until ready to eat. Go ahead and freeze those leftover breads; they easily reheat on the griddle right out of the freezer.

1 cup frozen shelled edamame, thawed

¾ cup warm water

1 cup spelt flour, plus more for dusting

1 teaspoon salt

2 tablespoons coconut oil, almost frozen (see sidebar, page 73)

2 scallions, finely chopped

CILANTRO MINT GARBANZO BEAN FLATBREADS

MAKES: 8 (6-INCH) FLATBREADS
TIME: ABOUT 1 HOUR, INCLUDING OIL FREEZING TIME

Flatbread is just pizza that needs a better bra. But this ultrahearty recipe gives flatbread all the texture it needs. I love the savory dough loaded with olive oil and savory garbanzo bean flour, but you can cut corners and use your favorite pizza dough and just shmear it all over with the cilantro basil pesto and roasted chickpeas. Want to spice them up some more? Serve them with *Creamy Tomato Tofu Curry* (page 183).

1 Make the dough first: In a large mixing bowl, combine the flours, baking powder, and salt. Spoon the almost frozen olive oil into the flour mixture and cut in with a pastry cutter or your fingers until the mixture looks like damp sand. Create a well in the center and pour in the water and lemon juice; stir to form a soft dough. Knead the dough on a lightly floured surface for a minute. If the dough seems sticky, sprinkle with flour; if it's too dry, sprinkle with water. Cover with a damp, clean kitchen towel and let the dough rest.

2 Preheat the oven to 450°F. Lightly oil a baking sheet or preheat a pizza stone.

3 While the oven preheats and the dough is resting, pulse together all the pesto ingredients, except the chickpeas, until smooth. Transfer to a mixing bowl and stir in the chickpeas.

WHOLE WHEAT OLIVE OIL CRUST

1½ cups whole wheat white flour, plus more for dusting

½ cup garbanzo bean flour

½ teaspoon baking powder

½ teaspoon salt

¼ cup olive oil, almost frozen (see sidebar, page 73)

¾ cup cold water

1 tablespoon freshly squeezed lemon juice

Olive or coconut oil, for pan (optional)

Cornmeal, for dusting

4 Divide the dough into eight equal pieces and dust generously with whole wheat flour. Shape each piece of dough into a ½-inch-thick round on a work surface generously dusted with cornmeal. Do this either with a rolling pin dusted with flour, or just pat the dough with your fingers.

5 Divide the pesto mixture evenly on top of each round, smoothing the pesto almost to the edges. Bake each mini pizza—wait, I mean FLATBREAD—(perhaps you can bake up to three at a time, depending on the size of your pan or baking stone) for 15 to 20 minutes, or until the dough is browned and the top is sizzling. Dust the hot flatbreads with nutritional yeast and red pepper flakes before serving.

PRO-TIP: *Ninja training stealing precious kitchen time? Then purchase a pound of whole wheat pizza dough and use in place of the homemade crust. If the dough is frozen or chilled, set on the countertop to warm up completely (at least 20 minutes) and soften the gluten strands for easier shaping.*

CILANTRO BASIL PESTO

1 bunch cilantro (about 2 cups lightly packed leaves)

1 bunch basil (about 2 cups lightly packed leaves)

Grated zest of 1 lemon

⅓ cup extra-virgin olive oil

1 teaspoon salt

1½ cups (1 [14-ounce] can) cooked chickpeas, drained and rinsed

TOPPING

Nutritional yeast

Red pepper flakes

CHEEZY HERB SCONES

BRP

MAKES: 12 DROP SCONES
TIME: ABOUT 45 MINUTES

You know this one will be fun because I spelled "cheese" with a z. That's right, a healthy, savory scone that is also playful, spicy, and golden yellow like your favorite childhood cheesy baked snacks. If your breakfast is turning into brunch, fill these scones with *Tempeh Bacon Strips* (page 55), a ripe tomato slice, and a few leaves of spinach or arugula.

1 Preheat the oven to 400°F. Line a baking sheet with parchment paper.

2 In a large bowl, stir together the flours, baking powder, baking soda, turmeric, paprika, garlic powder, cayenne, and salt. Form a well in the center of the flour mixture.

3 In a blender, pulse together the almost frozen oils, soy milk, brown rice protein powder, nutritional yeast, miso, and vinegar until smooth. Pour this mixture into the flour well, then add the herbs and jalapeños, if using. Stir together just enough to moisten the ingredients to create a soft dough. Do not overmix the dough.

4 Dust a work surface with a little extra flour, then turn out the dough onto the work surface. Divide the dough in half and shape each piece into a round just under an inch thick. Slice each round into six equal triangles (just like slicing a pie), and brush the tops with a little canola oil.

continued

1½ cups unbleached all-purpose flour, plus more for dusting

1 cup whole wheat white or whole-grain pastry flour

1 tablespoon baking powder

1 teaspoon baking soda

1 teaspoon ground turmeric

1 teaspoon ground sweet paprika

1 teaspoon garlic powder

¼ teaspoon cayenne pepper (or ½ teaspoon for maximum heat!)

½ teaspoon salt

¼ cup olive oil, almost frozen (see sidebar, page 73)

¼ cup refined coconut oil, almost frozen (see sidebar, page 73)

1¼ cup unsweetened, plain soy or almond milk

½ cup brown rice protein powder

(continued)

½ cup nutritional yeast

2 tablespoons white miso

1 tablespoon apple cider vinegar

½ cup finely chopped scallions or fresh herbs, such as cilantro, oregano, basil, chives

½ cup pickled jalapeño peppers or pitted olives, well drained and patted dry (optional)

Canola oil, for brushing scones

5 Transfer the scones to the prepared baking sheet. Bake for 20 to 22 minutes, or until lightly browned and firm. Serve hot, or when cool, split in half and toast on a griddle.

CHEEZY KALE SCONES

Make this variation and you'll have in your hands the #1 top hit favorite scone of my editor Renée and, well, probably of mine, too. They're also delightful to look at, with all that deep green kale folded into the orangey-cheezy scone dough.

Add 1 cup of finely chopped, firmly packed kale along with the herbs.

CRANBERRY ORANGE CHOCOLATE CHIP SCONES

BRP

MAKES: 10 WEDGE-SHAPED SCONES
TIME: ABOUT 45 MINUTES

Do you ever find yourself thinking, "I want orange! No, wait, I want cranberry! Hrngh, maybe I want chocolate!" and then feel bad because you can't decide? You're in luck because this scone satisfies all—and, bonus, with nuts, for even more of a protein bang.

1 Preheat the oven to 400°F. Line a baking sheet with parchment paper.

2 In a large bowl, stir together the flours, baking powder, baking soda, and salt. Form a well in the center of the flour mixture.

3 In a blender, pulse together the almost frozen oils, soy milk, orange juice, pea protein powder, organic sugar, and orange zest until smooth. Pour this mixture into the flour well, then add the cranberries, chocolate chips, and almonds. Stir together just enough to moisten the ingredients to create a soft dough. Do not overmix the dough.

4 Dust a work surface with a little extra flour, then turn out the dough onto the work surface. Divide the dough in half and shape each piece into a round just under an inch thick. Slice each round into six equal triangles (just like slicing a pie). Brush the tops with a little canola oil and dust with sugar.

5 Transfer the scones to the prepared baking sheet. Bake for 20 to 22 minutes, or until lightly browned and firm. Serve hot, or when cool, split in half and toast on a griddle.

1½ cups unbleached all-purpose flour, plus more for dusting

1 cup whole wheat white or whole-grain pastry flour

1 tablespoon baking powder

1 teaspoon baking soda

½ teaspoon salt

¼ cup refined coconut oil, almost frozen (see sidebar, page 73)

¼ cup canola oil, almost frozen (see sidebar, page 73)

½ cup unsweetened, vanilla or plain soy or almond milk

½ cup freshly squeezed orange juice

½ cup brown rice protein powder

⅓ cup organic sugar, plus more for dusting

Grated zest of 1 orange

½ cup dried cranberries

½ cup vegan chocolate chips

½ cup chopped roasted almonds or roasted, unsalted peanuts

Canola oil, for brushing

PROTEIN BAKERY BASKET

RASPBERRY LIME SCONES

Most important discovery ever: My favorite flavor of seltzer makes a delightful zesty scone.

Replace the lemon zest with the finely grated zest of one lime. Replace the blueberries with fresh raspberries.

BLUEBERRY LEMON PROTEIN SCONES

BRP

MAKES: 10 WEDGE-SHAPED SCONES OR 8 LARGE SCONES
TIME: 1 HOUR (INCLUDES OIL-CHILLING TIME)

This is one of those classic scones found everywhere. Well, not THIS blueberry scone. Because it's full of extra protein. That's why it's here, and should be in your belly, pronto. Beo, don't miss the raspberry lime version on page 90.

1 Preheat the oven to 400°F. Line a baking sheet with parchment paper.

2 In a large bowl, stir together the flours, baking powder, baking soda, and salt. Form a well in the center of the flour mixture.

3 In a blender, pulse together the almost frozen oils, soy milk, rice protein powder, organic sugar, lemon juice, vanilla, and lemon zest until smooth. Pour this mixture into the flour well, then add the frozen berries. Stir together just enough to moisten the ingredients to create a soft dough. Do not overmix the dough.

4 Dust a work surface with a little extra flour, then turn the dough onto the work surface. Divide the dough in half and shape half into a disk just under 1 inch thick. Slice each disk into six wedges. Transfer the wedges to the parchment paper. Brush the tops with canola oil and sprinkle them with sugar.

5 Bake for 20 to 22 minutes, or until lightly browned and firm. Serve warm, or split and toasted on a griddle.

1½ cups unbleached all-purpose flour, plus more for dusting

1 cup whole wheat white or whole-grain pastry flour

1 tablespoon

1 teaspoon baking soda

½ teaspoon salt

¼ cup refined coconut oil, almost frozen (see sidebar, page 73)

¼ cup canola oil, almost frozen (see sidebar, page 73)

1 cup unsweetened, plain soy or almond milk

½ cup brown rice protein powder

⅓ cup organic sugar, plus more for sprinkling

3 tablespoons freshly squeezed lemon juice

1 teaspoon pure vanilla extract

Grated zest of 1 lemon

1 cup frozen blueberries, kept frozen

Canola oil, for brushing

COCOA SCONE TOPPING

¼ cup coconut sugar

1 tablespoon raw cocoa powder

SCONES

1½ cups unbleached all-purpose flour, plus more for dusting

1 cup whole wheat white or whole-grain pastry flour

1 tablespoon baking powder

1 tablespoon espresso powder

1 teaspoon baking soda

1 teaspoon ground cinnamon

½ teaspoon ground ginger

½ teaspoon salt

¼ cup refined coconut oil, almost frozen (see sidebar, page 73)

¼ cup canola oil, almost frozen (see sidebar, page 73)

(continued)

PUMPKIN MOCHA LATTE PROTEIN SCONES

BRP

MAKES: 10 WEDGE-SHAPED SCONES OR 8 LARGE SCONES
TIME: ABOUT 45 MINUTES

Coffee-meets-pumpkin isn't just a very niche dating app, it's also the concept behind these caffeinated scones. This is a recipe for those of us who enjoy pumpkin spice for all seasons. Can't get behind pumpkin except in autumn? You're on the wrong side of history, my friend.

1 Preheat the oven to 400°F. Line a baking sheet with parchment paper.

2 Prepare the scone topping by pulsing together the coconut sugar and cocoa powder in a blender until fine and powdery. Tap into a small bowl and set aside.

3 Make the scones: In a large bowl, stir together the flours, baking powder, espresso powder, baking soda, cinnamon, ginger, and salt. Form a well in the center of the flour mixture.

4 In a blender, pulse together the almost frozen oils, soy milk, pumpkin puree, rice protein powder, organic sugar, and vanilla until smooth. Pour this mixture into the flour well, then add the chocolate chips. Stir together just enough to moisten the ingredients to create a soft dough. Do not overmix the dough.

5 Dust a work surface with a little extra flour, then turn out the dough onto the work surface. Divide the dough in half and shape each piece into a round just under an inch thick. Slice each round into six equal triangles (just like slicing a pie). Brush the tops with a little canola oil.

6 Transfer the scones to the prepared baking sheet. Bake for 20 to 22 minutes, or until lightly browned and firm. Let cool for 5 minutes, then sprinkle the tops with the scone topping.

PUMPKIN SPICE CRANBERRY SCONES

A more run of-the-mill pumpkin scone for conventional types, or if you're from Connecticut. Omit the espresso powder and add ½ teaspoon of freshly grated nutmeg to the flour mixture. Use ½ cup of dried cranberries in place of the chocolate chips. Omit the cocoa scone topping, or if desired, dust the tops of the scones with a little organic sugar before baking.

SCONES (continued)

½ cup unsweetened, plain soy or almond milk

½ cup canned pure pumpkin puree

½ cup brown rice protein powder

½ cup organic sugar

1 teaspoon pure vanilla extract

½ cup vegan chocolate chips

Canola oil, for brushing

CLASSIC HEMP PROTEIN BERRY MUFFINS

HPP

MAKES: 12 MUFFINS
TIME: LESS THAN 45 MINUTES

Coconut or olive oil cooking spray, for muffin tin

1¾ cups unsweetened soy milk

1 tablespoon apple cider vinegar

½ cup unflavored hemp protein powder

¼ cup canola oil

2 tablespoons ground flaxseeds

½ teaspoon pure vanilla or almond extract

1 cup unbleached all-purpose flour

½ cup whole wheat pastry flour

½ cup organic sugar

1 tablespoon baking powder

½ teaspoon ground cinnamon

½ teaspoon salt

1 cup frozen or fresh berries

You'll notice the recipe title doesn't say "blueberry," "raspberry," or "snozzberry"—and that's because this muffin is adaptable to whatever berry your heart desires. There is one key, though: If you're using frozen berries, DO NOT THAW. Keep them frozen right until you're ready to use them. If you thaw them first, they will be a mushy, puddly mess. And you cannot defeat your enemies with mushy, puddly muffins.

1 Preheat the oven to 350°F and lightly oil a 12-cup muffin tin.

2 Blend together the soy milk, apple cider vinegar, hemp protein powder, oil, ground flaxseeds, and vanilla until smooth.

3 In a large mixing bowl, combine the flours, organic sugar, baking powder, cinnamon, and salt and form a well in the center. Pour in the hemp milk mixture (make sure to scrape it all in; the muffins need every drop), and stir only enough to moisten; do not overmix! Fold in the berries, and use a large mechanical ice-cream scoop to evenly scoop the dough into the prepared muffin tin. Bake for 28 to 32 minutes, or until a toothpick inserted into the center of a muffin comes out clean; a few moist crumbs are okay.

continued

4 Remove from the oven, let cool in the tin for 10 minutes, then carefully transfer the muffins to a wire rack. Best served when allowed to cool for 20 minutes to help the muffins firm up a little.

CHOCOLATE CHIP MUFFINS

In the lost pages of muffin history someone brilliant, possibly not of this Earth due to the pure inspiration of it, tossed chocolate chips into humble muffin batter. You, too, can touch such greatness by leaving out the berries and replacing them with chocolate chips.

BAKERY-STYLE BLUEBERRY RICE PROTEIN MUFFINS

BRP **SP**

MAKES: 12 MUFFINS
TIME: 45 MINUTES

Okay, these are just your everyday blueberry muffins, plumped up with protein. They taste somewhat bakery bought and, yes, they're mainstream. You got a problem with fluffy, tender, crowd-pleasing blueberry muffins? Well, I don't care and muffin you say will change my mind.

1 Preheat the oven to 350°F and lightly oil a 12-cup muffin tin.

2 Blend together the soy milk, vinegar, brown rice protein powder, canola oil, flaxseeds, and vanilla until smooth.

3 In a large mixing bowl, combine the flours, organic sugar, baking powder, baking soda, cinnamon, and salt and form a well in the center. Pour in the hemp milk mixture (make sure to scrape it all in; the muffins need every drop), and stir only enough to moisten; do not overmix! Fold in the frozen or fresh berries, and use a large mechanical ice-cream scoop to evenly scoop the dough into the prepared muffin tin. Bake for 28 to 32 minutes, or until a toothpick inserted into the center of a muffin comes out clean; a few moist crumbs are okay.

4 Remove from the oven, let cool in the tin for 10 minutes, then carefully transfer the muffins to a wire rack. Best served when allowed to cool for 20 minutes to help the muffins firm up a little.

continued ➲

Coconut or olive oil cooking spray, for muffin tin

1¾ cups unsweetened soy or almond milk

1 tablespoon apple cider vinegar

½ cup unflavored brown rice protein powder

⅓ cup canola oil

2 tablespoons ground flaxseed, preferably golden flax

½ teaspoon pure vanilla extract

1 cup unbleached all-purpose flour

½ cup whole wheat pastry flour

½ cup organic sugar

1 tablespoon baking powder

½ teaspoon baking soda

½ teaspoon ground cinnamon

½ teaspoon salt

1½ cups frozen or fresh blueberries

PROTEIN BAKERY BASKET

NOTE

If you're using frozen berries, DO NOT THAW. Keep them frozen right until you're ready to use them, to avoid purple-streaked muffins. Also, if you can find golden flaxseed (grind your own if you can only get them whole), the blond color of the seeds blends seamlessly into the light-hued batter.

Here are two more totally sellout, everybody-likes-these flavor variations:

CRANBERRY WALNUT ORANGE MUFFINS

Omit the blueberries! Instead, stir into the batter the grated zest of one orange OR 1 teaspoon of orange extract, 1 cup of dried cranberries, and ½ cup of roughly chopped walnuts. Sprinkle the top of each muffin with a scattering of crushed walnuts.

LEMON PISTACHIO POPPY SEED MUFFINS

Tell those blueberries to find another muffin today. Instead, stir into the batter the grated zest of one lemon OR 1 teaspoon of lemon extract, ½ cup roughly chopped shelled pistachios, and 2 tablespoons of poppy seeds. Sprinkle the top of each muffin with a few chopped pistachios and a scattering of poppy seeds.

CHOCOLATE HEMP AVOCADO MUFFINS

HPP

MAKES: 12 MUFFINS
TIME: ABOUT 45 MINUTES

Avocado may not be the first ingredient that comes to mind with muffins (hey, it's second here, after all), but it adds a creaminess and structure to baked goods. Add chocolate and hemp and you've got a subtly rich muffin to keep you powered through the day.

1 Preheat the oven to 350°F and lightly grease a 12-cup muffin tin.

2 Combine the avocado, soy milk, flax seeds, vinegar, vanilla, and sugar in a blender or food processor fitted with the steel blade. Pulse until smooth. (Small flecks of avocado are okay! You may even *want* them there to add more avocado mystique.) Combine the flour, chocolate hemp powder, cocoa powder, baking powder, baking soda, and salt in a mixing bowl, and whisk well.

3 Use a large mechanical ice-cream scoop to evenly distribute the batter in the prepared muffin tin.

4 Bake for 25 to 30 minutes, or until a toothpick inserted into the center of a muffin comes out mostly clean; a few moist crumbs are okay. Let cool for about 5 minutes before removing from the tin. These muffins are best consumed the day they are made. Store leftovers in a tightly covered container in the refrigerator or freeze. Split and toast the muffins on a griddle for the best flavor.

PRO-TIP: *Chocolate hemp protein powder is simple flavored hemp powder that usually contains only hemp, coconut or palm sugar, and cocoa powder. If you'd rather use unflavored hemp protein powder, add 1 tablespoon of coconut sugar and 1 teaspoon of raw cocoa powder to the recipe.*

Coconut or olive oil cooking spray, for muffin tin

1 ripe Haas avocado, peeled and pitted

1½ cup unsweetened plain, vanilla, or chocolate soy or almond milk

2 tablespoons ground flaxseeds

1 tablespoon apple cider vinegar

1 teaspoon pure vanilla extract

⅔ cup coconut sugar

1 cup whole wheat pastry flour

½ cup chocolate hemp powder

⅓ cup Dutch-process cocoa powder

2 teaspoons baking powder

½ teaspoon baking soda

½ teaspoon salt

SUNSHINE CHIA CORN MUFFINS

BRP

MAKES: 12 MUFFINS
TIME: ABOUT 45 MINUTES

There's one in every crowd . . . but i don't judge (just eat a cupcake already, you philistine!). So, here is a recipe for the sweet muffin lovers out there and sneaking nutrition into the likes of you with chia seeds and brown rice protein.

1 Preheat the oven to 350°F and lightly oil a 12-cup muffin tin.

2 Make the topping: In a small cup, combine the topping ingredients.

3 Make the muffins: Blend together the soy milk, vinegar, brown rice protein powder, canola oil, and chia seeds until smooth.

4 In a large mixing bowl, combine cornmeal, flour, sugar, baking powder, and salt and form a well in the center. Pour in the soy milk mixture (make sure to scrape it all in; the muffins need every drop), and stir only enough to moisten; do not overmix! Use a large mechanical ice-cream scoop to evenly scoop the dough into the prepared muffin tin. Sprinkle the tops of the muffins with a pinch or two of topping.

5 Bake for 28 to 32 minutes, or until a toothpick inserted into the center of a muffin comes out clean; a few moist crumbs are okay.

6 Remove from the oven, let cool in the tin for 10 minutes, then carefully transfer the muffins to a wire rack. Best served when allowed to cool for 20 minutes to help the muffins firm up a little.

Coconut or olive oil cooking spray, for muffin tin

TOPPING

2 tablespoons cornmeal

1 teaspoon chia seeds

Pinch of salt

MUFFINS

2 cups unsweetened soy milk

2 tablespoons apple cider vinegar

½ cup unflavored brown rice protein powder

¼ cup canola oil

3 tablespoons chia seeds, preferably white chia

1¼ cups organic cornmeal

½ cup unbleached all-purpose flour

⅓ cup organic sugar

1 tablespoon baking powder

½ teaspoon salt

BANANA BUCKWHEAT BREAKFAST COOKIES

GF **LP** **NSP**

MAKES: 1 DOZEN LARGE COOKIES
TIME: 30 MINUTES OR LESS

There are junk food cookies you mindlessly shove into your mouth between six and eleven a.m. Then there are wholesome cookies that do your body some good, instead of hurtling your digestive system and the rest of your morning down the proverbial stairs. Don't treat your body like the pregnant lady in a terrible soap opera! Set an intention to start that day right with these toothsome pucks stuffed with hearty buckwheat flour, bananas, flax, coconut oil, coconut sugar, nuts, and fruits.

1 Preheat the oven to 350°F. Line baking sheets with parchment paper.

2 In a large mixing bowl, combine the mashed banana, ground flaxseeds, coconut oil, coconut sugar, and vanilla until smooth. In a separate bowl, stir together the buckwheat flour, hemp protein powder, whole wheat white flour, cinnamon, nutmeg, baking soda, and salt.

3 Stir the dry ingredients into the wet ingredients. Before the dough is completely moistened, add the nuts and dried fruits. Stir only enough to moisten everything; the dough will be very thick.

continued ➲

⅔ cup well-mashed ripe banana (about 2 small bananas)

3 tablespoons ground flaxseeds

¼ cup virgin coconut oil, melted

½ cup coconut sugar

½ teaspoon pure vanilla extract

¾ cup buckwheat flour

½ cup hemp protein powder

¼ cup whole wheat white flour or gluten-free flour blend

½ teaspoon ground cinnamon

¼ teaspoon freshly grated nutmeg

½ teaspoon baking soda

¼ teaspoon salt

½ cup pecan or walnut pieces or any mix of nuts, seeds, cacao nibs, etc.

¼ cup dried cherries, cranberries, or raisins

PROTEIN BAKERY BASKET

4 Divide the dough into twelve equal portions (about
¼ cup each), drop onto the prepared baking sheets,
and flatten slightly with your hand. For neater, cuter round
cookies, press a 2½-inch round biscuit cutter into each
mound of dough. Gather any scraps outside the cutter
and pack them on top of the cookie before removing the
cutter. Press a few chopped nuts or seeds on top of each
cookie to show you care.

5 Bake for 12 to 14 minutes, or until the edges just begin
to brown. Let cool on the baking sheets for 5 minutes,
then transfer to wire racks to cool completely.

6 Store in a loosely covered container, as these cookies
get rather soft if tightly covered. Or freeze immediately
and thaw on a countertop.

PRO-TIP: *These cookies are best when loaded
with seeds and nuts. I usually just pour an assort-
ment into a ½-cup measuring cup before mixing
into the dough. My favorites: pepitas, chopped
walnuts, cacao nibs, hemp seeds, slivered almonds, chopped Brazil nuts, or sunflower seeds.*

SUPER TOAST: SAVORY *and* SWEET

Toast is easy to love. Crispy and satisfying, it's the perfect fix when committing to a whole sandwich doesn't seem quite right. Finished with some high-protein toppings, toast is not just empty calories but the perfect in-between snack, obvious breakfast buddy, or light and substantial dinner fare.

Toast is also the perfect solution for busy days when I have to put off the joy of cooking for the acceptance of blending or mashing good-for-you ingredients together. These toppings are basically high-powered dips, slathered on hot crunchy bread and garnished with fresh veggies, fruits, or nuts and even cacao nibs.

Not surprisingly, a special toast recipe is only as good as the bread it's on. Choose your bread wisely: Opt for well-made breads with minimal ingredients and hearty crusts, and organic when possible. There's a whole new world of gluten-free breads out there for all those antigluten heads, too, so do your homework! I've suggested what type of bread goes best with each spread: semolina, rye, marble, big hunks of sunflower seeds and grains, sans gluten . . . it's all up to you, toast ninja!

EDAMAME & PEA AVOCADO TOAST

MAKES: ENOUGH FOR 4–6 AVERAGE-SIZE SLICES OF TOAST
TIME: 20 MINUTES OR LESS

Green stuff on toast is here to stay. Think of this as a toothsome take on classic avocado toast, boosted with a base of tasty edamame and green pea pesto.

1 Make the spread: In a large saucepan over medium heat, bring a quart of water to a boil. Stir in the frozen edamame and simmer for 4 minutes. Stir in the frozen peas, bring to a rapid simmer again, then remove from the heat and drain through a colander. Rinse well with cold water to stop the cooking and shake the colander to drain away any sneaky excess water.

2 In a food processor, pulse the edamame and peas with the olive oil, garlic, lemon juice, and salt. Pulse into a slightly chunky paste and taste: Season with a little more lemon juice, fresh ground pepper, or salt, if desired. Pulse in the chopped herbs.

3 Assemble the toast: Spread the hot toast with a thick layer of the spread and layer on the avocado slices, then red onion. Scatter with toasted pepitas, drizzle with olive oil, and finish with a sprinkle of smoked paprika and a scatter of zested lemon peel.

SPREAD

1 cup frozen, shelled edamame

1 cup frozen green peas

1 tablespoon olive oil

2 garlic cloves

2 tablespoons freshly squeezed lemon juice

½ teaspoon salt

Freshly ground black pepper

¼ cup roughly chopped fresh herbs (basil, cilantro, mint) or green scallion tops

TO ASSEMBLE

Hot sourdough, rye, or semolina toast

1 ripe avocado, peeled, pitted, and thinly sliced

Thinly sliced red onion

Toasted pepitas

Drizzle of good-quality olive oil

Sprinkle of smoked paprika

Thinly zested lemon peel

CHICKPEA PESTO TOMATO TOAST

MAKES: ABOUT 2 CUPS TOPPING
TIME: LESS THAN 15 MINUTES

There's something about basil pesto and summer. Enjoy these hearty chickpea toasts made with the best fresh basil and tomatoes the season can offer.

1 Make the spread: In a food processor, pulse the basil leaves, garlic, walnuts, olive oil, lemon juice, and salt into a smooth paste. Pulse into a thick paste, occasionally scraping down the sides of the processor bowl with a rubber spatula.

2 Add the chickpeas and pulse into a slightly chunky paste. Use immediately, or chill for at least 30 minutes for the flavors to develop. Keep chilled in a tightly covered container and use within a week.

3 To assemble: Slather the chickpea pesto onto the hot toast and layer each slice with arugula, tomato, and avocado. Finish with a sprinkle of lemon juice and a flourish of salt and twist of black pepper. Devour now!

SPREAD

2 cups lightly packed fresh basil leaves

2 garlic cloves, peeled

½ cup toasted walnuts

3 tablespoons good-quality olive oil

2 tablespoons freshly squeezed lemon juice

½ teaspoon salt

1 cup cooked chickpeas, drained and well rinsed

TO ASSEMBLE

Hot whole-grain, sourdough, or semolina toast

Baby arugula leaves

Thinly sliced ripe tomato

Sliced avocado

Freshly squeezed lemon juice

Salt and freshly ground black pepper

SUPER TOAST: SAVORY + SWEET

OVEN-ROASTED TOMATOES AND MUSHROOMS

1 pint cherry tomatoes

½ pound shiitake mushrooms

2 tablespoons soy sauce

2 tablespoons olive oil

PUB BEANS

2 tablespoons finely minced shallot

1 tablespoon olive oil

1 (14-ounce) can navy beans, drained and rinsed

½ cup dark ale or vegan vegetable broth

1 heaping tablespoon tomato paste

1 tablespoon organic molasses

1 teaspoon mustard powder

¼ teaspoon freshly ground black pepper

Big pinch of sea salt

(continued)

PUB BEANS ON TOAST

LP

SERVES: 4
TIME: 45 MINUTES

To make this British classic, you might think you'd just dump a can of beans on top of some bread. Well, hold on there, mate. These beans are dressed to the nines with molasses, shallots, and the ninja's secret weapon: dark ale. Couple the beans with roasted tomatoes and mushrooms and you've got breakfast, elevenses, tea, all the jolly day long.

1 Prepare the tomatoes and mushrooms: Preheat the oven to 350°F. Line a baking sheet with parchment paper. Slice the cherry tomatoes in half and spread on half of the parchment paper. Remove and discard the stems from mushrooms and slice any very large mushroom caps in half (the mushrooms should be bite-size). Sprinkle the tomatoes and mushrooms evenly with the soy sauce and olive oil and toss lightly to coat. Make sure to spread out the vegetables into one layer. Roast for about 20 minutes, stirring occasionally, until the tomatoes are sizzling and the mushrooms are golden. Turn off the oven but keep the vegetables inside to stay warm.

2 Prepare the beans: In a large saucepan over medium heat, sauté the shallots in the olive oil for about 2 minutes, until soft and golden. Add the remaining ingredients and simmer for about 10 minutes, stirring occasionally. The sauce should thicken up a little. Taste and add a little more ketchup or salt, if necessary.

3 To assemble: When the beans are ready, arrange the hot toast on serving plates. Top generously with the warm beans and arrange the roasted tomatoes, mushrooms, and onion slices on top. Serve immediately.

TO ASSEMBLE

1 small white onion, sliced paper thin

Hot whole wheat, multigrain, or sourdough toast

GINGER SQUASH ADZUKI TOAST

LP

MAKES: ABOUT 2 CUPS SPREAD
TIME: 15 MINUTES, NOT INCLUDING ROASTING SQUASH

Beans on toast isn't just a British flavor. Check out the Asian flavors here: A sweet and savory adzuki bean base is the perfect foil for spicy kimchi and crunchy black sesame seed gomasio.

1 Make the spread: In a large mixing bowl, mash together the mashed squash, tahini, lemon juice, tamari, ginger, and toasted sesame oil until combined; leave it a little bit chunky. Gently fold in the adzuki beans.

2 To assemble: Arrange the hot toast on serving plates, and slather the tops with the warm squash adzuki spread. Top with kimchi and sliced green scallion tops. Dust generously with black sesame gomasio. Serve immediately.

SPREAD

1 cup roasted, seeded, and roughly mashed winter squash, warm

2 tablespoons tahini

1 tablespoon freshly squeezed lemon juice

1 tablespoon tamari

1 teaspoon grated fresh ginger

½ teaspoon toasted sesame oil

½ cup cooked adzuki beans, drained and well rinsed

TO ASSEMBLE

Hot multigrain, pumpernickel, or sourdough toast

Vegan cabbage kimchi, drained and chopped

Green scallion tops, thinly sliced

Black sesame gomasio (recipe follows)

Black Sesame Gomasio

1 In a skillet over medium heat, toast the black sesame seeds until fragrant, stirring occasionally.

2 Pour into a food processor, add the sea salt, and pulse only enough until crumbly . . . don't overblend into sesame butter! You can also pound together the toasted seeds and salt with a mortar and pestle. Get out some aggression, build some muscle, and make something tasty!

PRO-TIP: *To roast any winter squash or smallish pumpkin, split in half and scoop out the seeds. Rub the interior with a little oil, place on a parchment paper-covered baking sheet and roast in a preheated 400°F oven until easily pierced with a fork (25 to 45 minutes, depending on the size of each half).*

BLACK SESAME
GOMASIO

½ cup black sesame
seeds

2 to 3 teaspoons
large-flake salt,
such as Maldon

WHITE BEAN & CASHEW RICOTTA TOAST

MAKES: ABOUT 2½ CUPS SPREAD
TIME: LESS THAN 30 MINUTES

I'm probably pushing the boundaries of what can be called a ricotta, but this satisfies my craving for a mellow, creamy spread—without the usual help of tofu—that plays well with fresh toppings, such as baby kale, arugula, and thinly sliced tomatoes or radishes or cucumber. Or go bold and use it as a base for sweet toast, too: sliced strawberries and chopped fresh mint, or a swirl of almond butter, chopped dates, and a dusting of cinnamon.

1 Make the spread: In a small bowl, combine the cashew pieces with hot water and soak for at least 20 minutes, or until the cashews are tender. Set aside 1 tablespoon of the soaking water and drain away the rest.

2 In a food processor, blend the drained cashews and the reserved soaking water into a thick, slightly grainy paste. Add the beans, olive oil, lemon juice, agave nectar, and salt. Pulse into a thick mixture, occasionally stopping to scrape down the sides of the processor bowl. Don't overblend; it's preferable that this have a somewhat grainy texture. Taste and add a pinch more salt, sugar, or lemon juice, if desired.

3 Use immediately, or chill for at least 30 minutes for the flavors to develop.

4 Slather over hot toast and top with either the savory or sweet garnishes.

SPREAD

½ cup unroasted cashew pieces

½ cup hot tap water

1 (16-ounce) can cannellini beans or navy beans, well drained and rinsed

2 teaspoons mild-flavored olive oil

2 teaspoons freshly squeezed lemon juice

½ teaspoon agave nectar

½ teaspoon salt

Hot whole-grain or sourdough toast

SAVORY GARNISHES

Baby kale leaves

Diced cherry tomatoes

Ground sweet paprika

Freshly ground black pepper

SWEET GARNISHES

Thinly sliced strawberries

Fresh mint leaves

Date syrup or pure maple syrup

Pink sea salt

SUPER TOAST: SAVORY + SWEET

2 teaspoons virgin coconut oil or olive oil

1 teaspoon black mustard seeds

1 (½-inch-thick) piece fresh ginger, peeled and minced

2 tablespoons minced shallots

1 hot red or green chile, minced (optional)

¾ cup uncooked red lentils, rinsed

2 teaspoons mild or hot curry powder

½ teaspoon salt

2 cups water

1 heaping teaspoon tomato paste

½ cup diced fresh tomatoes

TOPPING

1 pint cherry tomatoes, sliced in half

1 cup fresh cilantro leaves, roughly chopped

1 serrano or jalapeño pepper, minced

2 tablespoons freshly squeezed lemon juice

1 teaspoon garam masala, plus more for sprinkling

¼ teaspoon salt

Hot multigrain or sourdough toast

GARAM MASALA RED LENTIL TOAST

LP

MAKES: ABOUT 2 CUPS SPREAD
TIME: LESS THAN 30 MINUTES

Indian-style beans—more specifically lentils—on toast! Gently simmered creamy red lentils spiked with ginger and curry powder are great on seed-rich whole-grain toast, even better generously dusted with garam masala. Leftover lentils can be gently mashed with a little cilantro and spread chilled on hot toast later, or used as dip for veggies.

1 Heat the oil in a large saucepan over medium-high heat. Add the mustard seeds and fry until they just begin to pop. Stir in the minced ginger, shallots, and chile and fry, stirring occasionally, until the shallots are softened.

2 Stir in the lentils, curry powder, salt, water, and tomato paste. Turn up the heat to high and bring to a rolling boil for a minute, then lower heat to low. Cover and simmer for 15 to 20 minutes, or until the lentils are tender, creamy, and most of the water has been absorbed. The mixture should be like a thick sauce. Remove from the heat and stir in the diced tomatoes. Keep covered while you prepare the topping and toast.

3 Make the topping: In a mixing bowl, combine the cherry tomatoes, cilantro, serrano pepper, lemon juice, garam masala, and salt.

4 Arrange the hot toast on serving plates and slather the tops with the warm lentils. Top with the tomato salad and sprinkle with more garam masala. Serve immediately.

SPINACH DILL RICOTTA TOAST

MAKES: ABOUT 2 CUPS SPREAD
TIME: LESS THAN 30 MINUTES

Fresh Mediterranean-inspired flavor packed with protein and bold herbs. There's a little bit of ingredient prep required before smashing everything together into a tasty toast topper, but the efforts reward you with a hearty yet veggie-loaded light meal.

1 Heat a 10-inch skillet over medium-high heat. Add the spinach, 1 cup at a time, and stir it around; it will literally melt in volume. When all the spinach has been added, cover the pan and cook for 30 seconds. Remove the spinach from the skillet with a slotted spoon, and place it in a sieve. Press with the back of the spoon to extract as much liquid as possible. Spread out the spinach on a plate to cool, and when cool enough to handle chop it roughly. Set aside.

2 Crumble the pressed tofu into a food processor fitted with the steel blade. Add the beans, oil, garlic, lemon juice, oregano, salt, and dill. Pulse into a thick paste. Taste the mixture and season with a little more lemon juice or salt, if desired. Transfer to a mixing bowl and fold in the chopped cooked spinach.

3 Toast up that bread! Top your slices with a thick layer of the spread and layer over that slices of tomato, onion, and cucumber. Scatter with chopped dill, drizzle with olive oil, and finish with a bit of salt and black pepper.

PRO-TIP: For best results, press the tofu for 30 minutes: Slice tofu into 8 pieces, sandwich between 2 cutting boards, and press over a sink for 30 minutes. Or use a tofu press.

SPREAD

3 cups baby spinach leaves

1 pound firm tofu, pressed

1 cup cooked or canned white beans, such as cannellini or navy, drained and rinsed

1 tablespoon olive oil

2 garlic cloves, chopped

1 tablespoon freshly squeezed lemon juice

1 teaspoon dried oregano

½ teaspoon salt

⅓ cup chopped fresh dill

TO ASSEMBLE

Hot sourdough, rye, or semolina toast

Thinly sliced ripe tomato

Thinly sliced red onion

Thinly sliced hothouse cucumber

Chopped fresh dill

Drizzle of good-quality olive oil

Salt and freshly ground black pepper

CHOCOLATE HAZELNUT CHIKDATE TOAST

MAKES: ABOUT 1¼ CUPS SPREAD
TIME: LESS THAN 15 MINUTES

No, "chikdate" isn't the new Tinder. It is a splendid mash-up (literally) of chickpeas and dates. Add hazelnuts and cocoa powder and you've got the healthiest version of that ubiquitous chocolate hazelnut spread this side of the Italian Alps.

1 Make the spread: Place the dates in a bowl and pour in the boiling water. Cover the bowl and set the dates aside to soak for about 30 minutes, or until very soft and tender. Remove the dates from the soaking water but set the water aside for now. Remove and discard pits from the dates.

2 In a food processor, pulse the hazelnuts until finely ground. Add the softened dates and chickpeas. Pulse into a thick paste, occasionally scraping down the sides of the processor bowl with a rubber spatula.

3 Add the cocoa powder, vanilla, and salt. Pulse and scrape down the bowl until the cocoa powder is completely absorbed into the spread. If the spread seems too thick to blend, pulse in a tablespoon of date soaking water at a time until the desired consistency is reached. Depending on the moisture content of the dates, you may use up to 4 tablespoons of the soaking water.

continued ➲

SPREAD

10 Medjool dates

½ cup boiling water

½ cup roasted whole hazelnuts

½ cup cooked chickpeas, drained and well rinsed

3 rounded tablespoons raw cocoa powder

½ teaspoon pure vanilla extract

Big pinch of sea salt

TO ASSEMBLE

Hot whole-grain or oatmeal toast

Chopped toasted hazelnuts

Sliced bananas

Chopped dates or goji berries

Sprinkle of raw cocoa powder or freshly grated nutmeg

SUPER TOAST: SAVORY + SWEET

4 Use immediately, or scoop into a container, cover, and chill for at least 30 minutes for the flavors to develop. For best flavor, use within 3 days.

5 To assemble: Slather over the hot toast and top with the hazelnuts, banana, dates, and cocoa powder.

PRO-TIP: *Most hazelnuts are sold raw and you'll need to toast them at home. Spread unroasted nuts into a baking pan and roast for 10 to 15 minutes at 350°F until the skins crack and flake and the nuts begin to look golden. Remove from the oven, pour the hot nuts into a clean dish towel, and wrap the towel tightly into a bundle. Twist the bag several times to slough off the hazelnut skins. Open the bag, pick out the hazelnuts, and shake the towel outside your apartment window and shower your city with toasted hazelnut skins.*

SUPERFOOD CHOCOLATE ALMOND TOAST

 NSP

MAKES: ABOUT 1¼ CUPS SPREAD
TIME: LESS THAN 20 MINUTES

Chocolate and almonds. I once stated that I buckle when you wave that combo in my face (see page 21). Add to toast and just STOP. Not only does this topping have all the protein and nutrient goodness of the nuts, but it has the bonus of hemp and maca superfoods. As if chocolate and almonds weren't already spectacular.

SPREAD

1 cup roasted whole almonds

¼ cup shelled hemp seeds

¼ cup coconut sugar

¼ cup raw cocoa powder

3 tablespoons maca powder

¼ teaspoon sea salt

3 tablespoons melted virgin coconut oil

TO ASSEMBLE

Hot whole-grain or rustic white bread toast

Sliced strawberries or bananas, or fresh raspberries

Goji berries

Cacao nibs

1 Make the spread: In a food processor, pulse the almonds until finely ground. Add the hemp seeds. Pulse into a thick paste, occasionally scraping down the sides of the processor bowl with a rubber spatula.

2 Add the coconut sugar, cocoa powder, maca powder, and salt. Pulse and scrape down the bowl until the powders are completely absorbed into the spread. Pulse in the melted coconut oil.

3 Use immediately, or pack into a glass container, cover, and chill for at least 30 minutes for the flavors to develop. Keep chilled in a tightly covered container and use within 3 weeks. The chilled spread will be very firm; set it on a kitchen counter for 5 minutes to soften up a little for easier spreading.

4 To assemble: Slather over the hot toast and top with the fruit and cacao nibs, or eat with a spoon; toast doesn't care.

PROTEIN-PACKED PATTIES and BURGERS

There's nothing quite as polarizing yet alluring as a homemade veggie burger. Hated or loved, veggie burgers made from scratch rarely rate just a "meh"! There are a lot of bad veggie burgers committing crimes on innocents daily. Yet there are burgers that come to the rescue and renew our faith in something hearty yet animal-friendly to serve with lots of ketchup and pickles.

During my quest to develop convenient, easy-to-make-in-quantity, and compelling protein-packed vegan meals, creating a series of veggie burgers (and a few other similar recipes, such as balls and a veggie loaf) made brilliant sense. Unlike fleshy burgers, veggie burgers require a series of ingredients to make a truly satisfying bite.

All the better to make the most of real vegetables, legumes, nuts, soy foods, and even protein powders.

To my delight, the addition of plant-based protein powders not only increases the protein content, it helps the veggie burger hold together (no more crumbly, mushy burgers) AND gives them a springy, firm texture.

While these burgers have the muscle to withstand buns, bread, and all the burger fixin's, my kind of modern burger is not served on a bun, but on a bowl. Each burger here can be served as is or paired with a superloaded bowl complete with a starch, veggies, and the sauciest of sauces.

VEGGIE BURGER NINJA SCHOOL

Even though they're only patties of stuff smooshed together for delicious results, a few tips can make all the difference.

Cuter veggie burgers

Looks ain't everything, but sometimes perfectly round homemade veggie burgers provide a sense of instant accomplishment. And who couldn't use a little more of that in their lives?

To shape a lovely burger, pat ¼ to ⅓ cup of burger mixture into a disk about 1 inch thick. Press a large round cookie cutter into the mixture. Firmly pack any excess trimming on top of the burger before removing the cutter. A 4-inch cutter makes a massive all-American restaurant-size burger, and a 3- to 3-½ inch cutter builds smaller-portioned burgers for a few more burgers per recipe.

Bake or fry

Most of these burgers are baked, but you can also fry them! For best results, use a well-seasoned cast-iron pan, medium heat, and generous slick of high-heat-friendly vegetable oil (such as peanut or high-heat refined canola). These burgers will take a little bit of time to cook all the way through, roughly 6 to 7 minutes per side. Use a wide, thin spatula and your most ninjalike wrist action when flipping these burgers, to prevent breakage.

Freeze!

You can freeze veggie burgers. Cook first, let them cool, then arrange in a single layer in a baking sheet that can slide easily into your freezer. Once frozen solid, pack between sheets of waxed or parchment paper and tightly seal in resealable plastic bags.

SUPER HEMP PROTEIN BEET BURGERS

GF   **HPP**

MAKES: 8 LARGE BURGERS
TIME: ABOUT 1 HOUR

This bold, beety burger is stoked with smoked paprika. If you're looking for a hearty patty that's ideal served with crisp vegetables and creamy dressing, this is your guy, er, burger. And speaking of dressing? *Dill Pickle Thousand Island Cashew Dressing* (page 148) is a great burger-building sauce.

1 Start the burgers: In a large saucepan, combine the broth, lentils, and thyme. Bring to a rolling boil, lower the heat to low, cover, and simmer for 30 minutes, or until tender but not overly mushy. Remove from the heat, uncover, and set aside to cool.

2 While the lentils cool, preheat the oven to 400°F, line a large baking sheet with parchment paper, and spray six large circles onto the paper with cooking oil spray.

3 Stir together the coating ingredients in a shallow bowl.

4 In a large mixing bowl, combine the lentils with all the remaining burger ingredients (but not the coating). Use your hands to knead the ingredients together to form a soft, moist mixture. If the mixture is overly wet, sprinkle in an additional tablespoon at a time of oats until the mixture is no longer soggy but still is moist.

continued ➲

BURGERS

1½ cups vegan vegetable broth

½ cup dried brown or black lentils

2 teaspoons dried thyme

Olive oil cooking spray, for brushing

1 cup finely chopped yellow onion

½ pound beets, peeled and shredded (1 very large beet, about 5 inches wide)

½ cup hemp protein powder

⅓ cup old-fashioned rolled oats, plus more oats for firmer burgers

½ cup walnut pieces, finely chopped

2 tablespoons all-natural ketchup

1 tablespoon olive oil

1 tablespoon smoked sweet paprika

1 teaspoon dried oregano

(continued)

½ teaspoon freshly
ground black pepper

¾ teaspoon salt,
or to taste

COATING

¾ cup old-fashioned
rolled oats

2 tablespoons shelled
hemp seeds

1 teaspoon smoked
paprika

½ teaspoon salt

5 Divide the mixture into eight balls and drop each ball into the coating mixture, gently rolling the ball to completely coat. Place each ball on an oiled circle on the parchment paper, then shape each into a patty about ½ inch thick. Spray generously with additional cooking oil and bake for 15 minutes, remove from the oven, and flip. Bake for another 10 to 15 minutes, or until the outside is crusty and the insides of the patties are piping hot.

TOMATO ZUCCHINI DILL BURGERS

GF HPP SP

MAKES: 8 BURGERS
TIME: ABOUT AN HOUR

Dive into the dreamy Aegean flavors of these springy zucchini patties crafted for a Hercules or Xena Warrior Princess (that's you). Enjoy heroically with Creamy with *Creamy Cucumber Garlic Dressing* (page 148).

1 Preheat the oven to 400°F and line a baking sheet with parchment paper. Generously brush eight circles of olive oil, about 4 inches wide and an inch apart, onto the paper where you'll shape the burgers.

2 Stir together the coating ingredients in a shallow bowl.

3 Make the burgers: Crumble the pressed tofu into the bowl. Add the remaining burger ingredients (but not the coating) and knead vigorously to combine everything into a stiff mixture. Taste and add a little extra salt, black pepper, or a dash of lemon juice, if desired.

4 Divide the mixture into eight balls and drop each ball into the coating mixture, gently rolling the ball to completely coat. Place each ball on an oiled circle on the parchment paper, then shape each into a patty about 1 inch thick. Spray the tops of the patties with more cooking spray, or drizzle with oil.

5 Bake for 15 minutes, then remove from the oven and carefully flip each burger over. Bake for another 10 minutes or until the coating is golden brown. Serve hot or warm, as desired, on small slider-size vegan burger buns or instead of falafel, use on the *Falafel Bowl with Lemon Roasted Potatoes, Basil Lemon Cashew Dressing, and Chopped Mediterranean Salad* (page 155).

Olive oil, for brushing

COATING

⅓ roughly chopped walnuts

⅓ cup vegan panko or gluten-free bread crumbs

1 teaspoon dried thyme

½ teaspoon salt

BURGERS

1 pound extra-firm tofu, pressed (see pro-tip, page 114)

1 cup chopped fresh dill

4 scallions, white and green parts, minced

2 garlic cloves, peeled and minced

1 cup firmly packed grated zucchini

1 cup grated carrot

1 cup diced and seeded fresh tomato

1 tablespoon olive oil

½ cup hemp protein powder

1 tablespoon dried oregano

1 teaspoon salt

Olive oil cooking spray, for brushing

About ½ teaspoon freshly ground black pepper

Freshly squeezed lemon juice (optional)

Olive oil cooking spray or olive oil, for brushing

COATING

1 cup old-fashioned rolled oats

3 tablespoons sunflower seeds

Big pinch of salt

BURGERS

1 pound extra-firm tofu, drained and pressed (see pro-tip, page 114)

1 yellow onion, peeled and finely minced

2 garlic cloves, peeled and minced

3 tablespoons sunflower butter

3 tablespoons tomato paste

½ cup old-fashioned rolled oats

1½ teaspoons smoked paprika

1 teaspoon dried thyme

1 teaspoon dried oregano

1 teaspoon salt

½ teaspoon freshly ground black pepper

Tomato paste (optional)

SUNNY OAT BURGERS

MAKES: 8 PATTIES
TIME: 1 HOUR

These tofu burgers are loaded with earthy goodness: sunflower seeds, oats, and sunflower butter. Grill leftover patties until hot and top with avocado and grated carrot for a mellow yet sturdy breakfast for hectic weekday mornings.

1 Preheat the oven to 400°F and line a baking sheet with parchment paper. Generously brush six circles of olive oil, about 4 inches wide and an inch apart, onto the paper where you'll shape the burgers.

2 Stir together the coating ingredients in a shallow bowl.

3 Make the burgers: Crumble the pressed tofu into a large mixing bowl. Add the remaining burger ingredients (but not the coating) and knead vigorously to combine everything into a stiff mixture. Taste and add a little extra salt, pepper, or even a spoonful of tomato paste, as desired.

4 Divide the mixture into eight balls and drop each ball into the coating mixture, gently rolling the ball to completely coat. Place each ball on an oiled circle on the parchment paper, then shape each into a patty about 1 inch thick. Spray the tops of the patties with additional cooking spray, or drizzle with oil.

6 Bake for 15 minutes, remove from the oven, and carefully flip each burger over. Bake for another 12 to 15 minutes, or until the oats and sunflower seeds are golden brown. Serve hot or warm with ketchup, mustard, vegan mayo, or on the *Green Goddess Burger & Roasted Potatoes Bowl* (page 147).

BLACK BEAN HEMP BURGERS

HPP **LP**

MAKES: 8 BURGERS
TIME: ABOUT 1 HOUR, INCLUDING ROASTING SWEET POTATO

Black bean burgers are a pantry staple great for any occasion, and an easy sell for omnivores, too. This version is unusual in a few ways even beyond the addition of hemp protein: The mixture is moistened with roasted sweet potato and rolled in a crunchy coating of crushed tortilla chips and pepitas, but perhaps the most remarkable twist is the roasting of the cooked black beans, a tip I learned from The Serious Eats blogger.

Roasting the beans (either home cooked, or more likely for busy protein nerds like us, canned) adds a new dimension of hearty, chewy texture by drying them out a bit for a denser, meaty consistency, and deepening the earthy character of the beans with roasted notes. I'm not one to waste making the most of a hot oven: While the beans roast, you'll also toast shelled pumpkin seeds for even more roasted flavor in the burger mixture.

1 Start the burgers: Line a large baking sheet with parchment paper. Spread the rinsed beans in a single layer over half of the baking sheet, and spread the pepitas on the other side. Preheat the oven to 400°F. While the oven is preheating, place the sheet with the beans and pepitas in the oven and roast for about 10 minutes, or until the beans look dry and the skins start to break on the outside, and the pepitas are golden. Remove from the oven and transfer the beans to a mixing bowl. Roughly chop the pepitas and add them to the beans.

continued ➲

BURGERS

1 (14-ounce) can black beans, drained and rinsed

½ cup pepitas

1 pound sweet potato (1 [8-inch] sweet potato), roasted in the skin until soft

1 large yellow onion, peeled and finely chopped

2 garlic cloves, peeled and minced

1 jalapeño pepper, seeded (or leave the seeds for a hotter burger) and minced

½ cup unflavored hemp protein powder

2 teaspoons ancho chile powder

1 teaspoon ground cumin

1 teaspoon salt

Olive oil cooking spray, for brushing

COATING

2 cups finely crushed blue or yellow corn tortilla chips

3 tablespoons pepitas, roughly chopped

2 Peel the roasted sweet potato, transfer to bean mixture, add the remaining burger ingredients, except the cooking oil spray, and mash everything together into a soft, moist mixture.

3 With the cooking oil spray, spray eight large circles.

4 Stir together the coating ingredients in a shallow bowl.

5 Divide the mixture into eight balls and drop each ball into the coating mixture, gently rolling the ball to completely coat. Place each ball on an oiled circle on the parchment paper, then shape each into a patty about ½ inch thick. Spray with a little additional oil and bake for 15 minutes, remove from the oven, and flip. Bake for another 10 to 15 minutes, or until the burgers are firm and the insides of the patties are piping hot.

PRO-TIP: *Roast the sweet potato whole on a rimmed baking sheet in a preheated 400°F oven until easily pierced with a fork. While it's roasting, chop the rest of the veggies and prepare the beans and pepitas for roasting. Then crush the tortilla chips; I just leave them in the bag and crush the bag with my hands or a rolling pin. When the sweet potato is ready, slice in half to speed up the cooling and use when it's cool enough to handle, about 5 minutes.*

GREEN GODDESS BURGERS

GF **HPP** **SP**

MAKES: 8 BURGERS
TIME: ABOUT AN HOUR

For fresh tofu burgers loaded with fistfuls of fresh green herbs and spinach, and crusted with hemp and pumpkin seeds, these have a surprisingly toothsome firmness. They're great on a salad or with roasted potatoes, and with any creamy, bright dressing.

1 Preheat the oven to 400°F and line a baking sheet with parchment paper. Generously brush eight circles of olive oil, about 4 inches wide and an inch apart, onto the paper where you'll shape the burgers.

2 Stir together the coating ingredients in a shallow bowl.

3 Make the burgers: Steam the spinach until tender and wilted but still bright green. When it's cool enough to handle, gather and squeeze out as much water as possible and press into a dense ball. Finely chop the spinach and transfer to a mixing bowl.

4 Crumble the pressed tofu into the bowl with the spinach. Add the remaining burger ingredients (but not the coating) and knead vigorously to combine everything into a stiff mixture. Taste and add a little extra salt, black pepper, or dash of lemon juice, if desired.

continued ➲

Olive oil cooking spray or olive oil, for brushing

COATING

⅓ cup hemp seeds

⅓ cup roughly chopped pepitas

1 teaspoon dried thyme

½ teaspoon salt

BURGERS

½ pound spinach, stemmed

1 pound extra-firm tofu, pressed (see pro-tip, page 114)

1 cup chopped fresh parsley

1 cup chopped fresh cilantro

¼ cup finely chopped fresh mint or chives

4 scallions, white and green parts, minced

2 garlic cloves, peeled and minced

2 tablespoons freshly squeezed lemon juice

1 tablespoon olive oil

(continued)

BURGERS (continued)

½ cup walnut pieces, coarsely ground

½ cup hemp protein powder

1 teaspoon salt

About ½ teaspoon freshly ground black pepper

Freshly squeezed lemon juice (optional)

5 Divide the mixture into eight balls and drop each ball into the coating mixture, gently rolling the ball to completely coat. Place each ball on an oiled circle on the parchment paper, then shape each into a patty about 1 inch thick. Spray the tops of the patties with more cooking oil spray, or drizzle with oil.

6 Bake for 15 minutes, then remove from the oven and carefully flip each burger over. Bake for another 10 minutes, or until the coating is golden brown. Serve hot or warm with your favorite guacamole or guess which bowl . . . the *Green Goddess Burger & Roasted Potatoes Bowl* (page 147).

VEGETABLE KORMA TOFU PATTIES

MAKES: 8 PATTIES
TIME: ABOUT 1 HOUR

Curry + burger = love. These chewy cashew and tofu burgers are inspired by the subtly spicy flavors of Indian vegetable korma, a delightful dish of vegetables simmered in a creamy sauce, if you've never known it. The crunchy coconut mustard seed coating takes it to an even higher level.

1 Preheat the oven to 400°F, line a large baking sheet with parchment paper, and spray six large circles onto the paper with cooking oil spray.

2 Stir together the coating ingredients in a shallow bowl.

3 Make the burgers: While the oven preheats, soak the cashews with the hot water in a small bowl for 20 minutes, until soft and plump. Do not drain the cashews. Pour the cashews and water into a blender, add the tomato paste, and pulse until smooth and creamy.

4 Heat the coconut oil over medium heat in a large, heavy skillet. Add the mustard seeds, cook until they pop, then stir in the curry powder. Remove from the heat and use a rubber spatula to scrape into a mixing bowl. Add the onion, tofu, pea protein powder, cauliflower, peas, cilantro, and salt. Stir in the cashew puree and knead to combine everything into a thick mixture that is firm but somewhat moist.

continued

Olive oil spray or olive oil, for brushing

COATING

½ cup finely grated coconut

1 tablespoon black mustard seeds

½ teaspoon ground turmeric

½ teaspoon salt

BURGERS

½ cup unroasted cashews

½ cup hot tap water

2 tablespoons tomato paste

1 tablespoon virgin coconut oil

2 teaspoons black mustard seeds

2 teaspoons curry powder

1 large yellow onion, peeled and diced

1 pound extra-firm tofu, drained, pressed, crumbled (see pro-tip, page 114)

(continued)

BURGERS (continued)

½ cup pea protein powder

½ pound cauliflower, finely chopped (about ½ small head)

1 cup frozen green peas

1 cup roughly chopped fresh cilantro

1 teaspoon salt

5 Divide the mixture into eight balls and drop each ball into the coating mixture, gently rolling the ball to completely coat. Place each ball on an oiled circle on the parchment paper, then shape each into a patty about 1 inch thick. Spray the tops of the patties with additional cooking spray, or drizzle with oil.

6 Bake for 15 minutes, then remove from the oven and carefully flip each burger over. Bake another 10 minutes or until coconut coating is golden brown. Serve hot or warm, as desired, or in the *Korma Burger with Coconut Quinoa & Spinach Salad* (page 149).

PINTO BBQ SEITAN BURGERS

MAKES: 4 REALLY BIG AMERICAN-SIZE BURGERS OR 6-8 SMALLER UN-AMERICAN BURGERS
TIME: ABOUT 1 HOUR

When I think America, I think BBQ. (I also think sportball, reality TV, and riding John Deere tractors across the Grand Canyon in an American flag bikini top, listening to a Van Halen song, while eagles soar above. But back to BBQ!) These beany, wheat-gluteny burgers don't require any additional protein and they're sturdy enough for even the firmest buns. (Go ahead, laugh: Heh-heh, firm buns.)

1 In a mixing bowl, slightly mash the pinto beans; keep them chunky. Add all the remaining ingredients, except the vital wheat gluten and oil for the pan, and stir to combine.

2 Now, knead in the vital wheat gluten about ¼ cup at a time. Crumble and break apart the mixture to help develop those meaty, all-American gluten strands. Form four balls for big burgers or six to eight for petite burgers.

3 Preheat a cast-iron pan over medium-low heat and oil lightly. To shape a burger, pat it down to about 1 inch thick on a work surface and shape with a ring mold to your desired size. Don't remove the mold this time: Lift the burger in the mold and place the whole thing in the pan. Fry for about 2 minutes, twist off the mold, and shape another burger as this one cooks in the pan. Cook each burger for 4 to 6 minutes per side, flipping once, or until both sides are well browned and the insides are completely cooked through. Occasionally spin each burger in the pan to ensure even cooking.

continued ➲

1 (14-ounce) can pinto beans, drained and rinsed

1 large yellow onion, peeled and grated

2 garlic cloves, minced

1 tablespoon olive oil

½ cup vegan vegetable broth

2 tablespoons tomato paste

2 tablespoons soy sauce

1 tablespoon blackstrap molasses

2 teaspoons smoked sweet paprika

1 teaspoon ground cumin

½ teaspoon liquid smoke

1 teaspoon salt

½ cup vegan whole wheat bread crumbs

¾ cup vital wheat gluten

Olive or vegetable oil, for pan

4 Serve hot on toasted buns with all the proper fixin's (ketchup and sliced tomatoes), or in the *Pinto BBQ Burger Bowl with Succotash Sauté and Roasted Red Pepper Dressing* (page 153).

PRO-TIP: *Did you see what I did here . . . I fried these burgers! Unlike so many of the recipes in this chapter, pan frying really enhances the smoky flavor of these chewy burgers. But if you must bake instead of fry, opt to roll the burgers in a coating and spritz with oil. My preferred coating for this is the tortilla chip coating used for the Black Bean Hemp Burgers on page 129, then shape and bake the burgers as directed there.*

LENTIL WALNUT LOAF

PPP   LP

SERVES: 6-8
TIME: 2 HOURS

The classic vegan loaf becomes the perfect protein sandwich filling or snack. This is designed to be chilled and sliced for your midweek sandwich and snacking needs, but it's ready to meet your parents for Sunday night supper in the *Lentil Walnut Loaf Sunday Night Roast Bowl* (page 158). After all, even ninjas need to loaf around.

3 cups vegan vegetable broth

1 cup brown lentils

½ cup uncooked short-grain brown rice

1 teaspoon dried thyme

1 teaspoon paprika

½ teaspoon ground cumin

3 tablespoons olive oil, plus more for brushing

2 cups sliced cremini or button mushrooms

3 garlic cloves, chopped

1 carrot, grated

2 celery ribs, finely chopped

½ cup pea protein powder

¼ cup tamari

½ teaspoon freshly ground black pepper

⅓ cup rolled oats

1 cup walnuts, toasted and roughly chopped

1 Bring 2½ cups of the broth to a boil in a saucepan over high heat. Add the lentils, brown rice, thyme, paprika, and cumin. Continue to boil for about 2 minutes, then lower the heat to low, cover the pan, and simmer for 35 to 40 minutes, or until the lentils are mostly tender and the brown rice is tender but still chewy. Remove the pan from the heat, pour the mixture into a large mixing bowl, and set aside to cool (uncovered) for 20 minutes.

2 Preheat the oven to 350°F and line a 9 x 5 x 3-inch loaf pan with foil. Brush the foil with olive oil.

3 While the lentils and rice cook, prepare the vegetables. Heat 2 tablespoons of the olive oil in a large skillet over medium-high heat. Add the mushrooms and cook, stirring frequently, for 3 minutes, or until they begin to soften. Divide the mushrooms in half, and set aside. Heat the remaining tablespoon of oil in the skillet over medium heat, and add the garlic, carrot, and celery. Cook, stirring frequently, for 3 minutes, or until the vegetables are soft.

Add half the mushrooms to the skillet, and then combine the vegetables with the cooled lentil and rice mixture. Add the pea protein powder, tamari, pepper, oats, and walnuts to the bowl. Stir well (hands are still the best tool for this). Taste the dough and season with a little more tamari, if desired. Add the remaining ½ cup of broth, 1 tablespoon at a time, if the mixture seems dry.

4 Pack the mixture evenly into the prepared loaf pan. Spread the remaining mushrooms over the top of the loaf and brush generously with olive oil. Cover the pan tightly with foil and bake on the center rack for 40 minutes. Remove the foil and bake for another 15 to 20 minutes, or until the mushrooms are roasted and the edges look crisp.

5 Remove the loaf from the oven, uncover, and cool for about 5 minutes before serving. Let the loaf cool completely before refrigerating the remainder, tightly wrapped in plastic wrap, for sandwiches, toast topping, snacks, or sharing with strangers on the bus ride home.

CHICKPEA EGGPLANT HEMP VEGGIEBALLS & SIMPLE SPICY TOMATO SAUCE

PPP **LP**

MAKES: ABOUT 2½ DOZEN BALLS AND 2 QUARTS SAUCE
TIME: 1 HOUR

Get ballsy with this dish inspired by a Mark Bittman recipe for meat eaters trying to eat like vegans. Roasted eggplant and pea protein tenderize the vegan house favorite: baked chickpea meatballs. These balls are able to withstand a complete dousing of the homemade tomato sauce that's simple enough to make you'll feel like a jerk for buying tomato sauce in a jar. The sauce is tasty as is, but might just be illegally good with a handful of fresh basil or cilantro leaves stirred in immediately after cooking.

CHICKPEA EGGPLANT HEMP VEGGIEBALLS

1½ pounds purple eggplant, preferably long, thin eggplants

2 tablespoons olive oil

1 teaspoon salt

1 (14-ounce) can chickpeas, drained and rinsed

⅓ cup pea protein powder

1 large yellow onion, peeled and finely chopped

1 heaping tablespoon tomato paste

2 teaspoons dried oregano

1 teaspoon ground smoked paprika

½ cup vegan fine-textured, dried white or whole wheat bread crumbs

Olive oil cooking spray or olive oil, for brushing

1 Make the veggieballs: Preheat the oven to 400°F and line a large baking sheet with parchment paper. Do not peel the eggplant. Dice into 1-inch pieces. Transfer the eggplant to the baking sheet and toss with the olive oil. Sprinkle with a little of the salt and roast for 20 minutes, stirring occasionally, until the eggplant is tender and golden. Remove from the oven and let cool for 10 minutes, or until cool enough to handle.

2 Meanwhile, get that tomato sauce going! In a large saucepan over medium heat, sauté together the onion, garlic, and olive oil until the onion is soft and translucent. Stir in the remaining sauce ingredients except for the fresh basil/cilantro and bring to an active bubbling simmer, stirring occasionally. Lower the heat to low, partially cover the

pan, and continue to simmer for another 10 minutes, or until thickened slightly. If desired, pulse the sauce with an immersion blender to smooth it out a little, but leave it a little bit chunky. Turn off the heat and stir in the chopped basil or cilantro.

3 In a large mixing bowl, mash the chickpeas with a potato masher or your hands into a chunky paste. Add the cooled roasted eggplant and the remaining veggieball ingredients, except the cooking oil spray. Knead vigorously with your hands into a thick mixture. Lower the oven temperature to 375°F.

4 Lightly spray or brush with oil the same baking sheet used for roasting the eggplant. Use a mechanical ice-cream scoop to scoop out meatball-size portions onto the sheet, then lightly spray all the balls with additional cooking oil spray. Roast at 375°F for 20 minutes, or until the outside of the balls are golden and slightly crisp, and the interior is hot. Halfway through roasting, flip the balls over and spray or drizzle with a little more olive oil. Serve hot with tomato sauce over your favorite high-protein pasta or with the roasted broccoli from the *Pro Mac with Roasted Broc* (page 181).

SIMPLE & SPICY TOMATO SAUCE

1 large yellow onion, peeled and diced

4 garlic cloves, smashed

1 tablespoon olive oil

1 (28-ounce) can crushed or diced tomatoes, preferably fire-roasted

1 teaspoon red pepper flakes

1 teaspoon dried thyme

½ teaspoon salt

Freshly ground black pepper

½ cup roughly chopped fresh basil or cilantro

BAKED GREEN FALAFEL WITH PEA PROTEIN

MAKES: 2 DOZEN FALAFEL BALLS

TIME: 1 HOUR, NOT INCLUDING SOAKING CHICKPEAS

1 cup dried chickpeas

1 cup lightly packed chopped fresh parsley

½ cup lightly packed chopped fresh cilantro

4 garlic cloves, peeled

1 large white onion, peeled and chopped

3 tablespoons olive oil

2 tablespoons freshly squeezed lemon juice

1 teaspoon ground coriander

1 teaspoon ground cumin

½ teaspoon cayenne pepper

¾ teaspoon salt

½ teaspoon baking soda

½ cup pea protein powder

Olive oil cooking spray or olive oil, for brushing

Proper falafel must be green: Green means it's loaded with lots of tasty fresh parsley and cilantro, which make everything better. So, yes . . . MUST. If it's not green, you have made terrible life choices. Speaking of which, you have ten hours while the chickpeas soak to think about what you're doing with your life. Even if you do this overnight (a wise choice; good work!), have you thought about going back to school? Maybe you should get that raised freckle checked out. When's the last time you called your parents? Why do people deep-fry falafel when it's so much better baked?

1 Cover the chickpeas with 3 inches of cold water and soak for 8 to 10 hours; I like to do this in the morning before leaving for work, or playing hooky, or whatever you do with your days. Drain and discard the water.

2 Preheat the oven to 400°F and line a large baking sheet with parchment paper. In a food processor, grind the chickpeas with the parsley, cilantro, garlic, onion, olive oil, lemon juice, coriander, cumin, cayenne, salt, and baking soda into a thick, chunky paste. Add the pea protein powder and pulse until the powder is absorbed and the mixture is thickened. Taste and season with a little more salt and cayenne, if desired.

3 Scoop 2 tablespoon–size balls of the mixture onto the baking sheet. I use a medium-size mechanical cookie scoop for easy, neat scooping and shaping of falafel balls. Spray or brush each ball with olive oil and bake the falafel for 22 to 24 minutes, or until firm and the bottoms are golden brown. Serve hot with the sauce from the *Falafel Bowl with Lemon Roasted Potatoes, Basil Lemon Cashew Dressing, and Chopped Mediterranean Salad* (page 155), or go ahead and make the bowl and serve falafel as nature intended.

BETTER THAN EVER
BURGER BOWLS

Eating food out of bowls isn't a new thing, but it seems to be THE thing in these mid-2010s. My completely unscientific and hardly researched take on it: Until very recently, Westerners ate only singular portions of soup, oatmeal, or cornflakes out of miserable little bowls. Everything else, slap it on a plate. Usually this meant a hunk of animal fresh in the middle framed by a few overboiled, colorless vegetable garnishes. A travesty.

With more plant-based foods moving in and shaking up the system, that dinnertime tyrant, the big huge dinner plate, seems dated and unwieldy. How I am supposed to get quinoa, tahini sauce, kale, and tofu into my mouth when a fork just chases everything off the edge of this plate and onto the table? Dinner plates, my ninjas, are the other silent enemy (after rival ninja clans).

What does all this mean? Yes, burger and bowls. The best way to get your veggies and proteins in one fell swoop. And if you are a salad eater at heart, bowls loaded with leafy, crunchy, raw veggies topped with a hearty hot burger are the ultimate dinner companion. I could probably eat this way every day, and very often I do.

Bowls are fun to order in restaurants, but at home they admittedly can take a bit longer, as they require making two to four smaller recipes to build one meal. Following are some tips for streamlining your workflow to enjoy more bowls, as these are some of my favorite ways to consume a healthy balance of protein foods and fresh produce.

Most of the recipes here that go into making these bowls make plenty of food, for three very hungry people or four average appetites. Or they will make dinner for two and some nice leftovers for a few days of excellent lunch.

Burger Bowls

- Prepare the dressings the day before and keep chilled until ready to use.

- Prep the fresh vegetables right after shopping. Wash and spin dry greens and pack into airtight containers.

- Most of the burger mixtures can be made in advance and kept refrigerated for up to 2 days. Shape and bake as needed, or make the whole batch at once for leftovers.

Collard Green Wraps, the Single-Handed Salad

- Use collard greens as crunchy, ultra-low-calorie alternatives to whole wheat wraps.

- Select large, firm, fresh organic collard leaves.

- Trim the stems, then use a vegetable peeler or paring knife to trim the bulk away from the stem embedded in the leaf to make rolling it up easier.

- Slice burgers into strips to pile more easily into rolls.

- Don't forget the burrito-style roll to prevent fillings from falling out: fold the right and left sides toward the center first, then roll up the leaf away from the stem end.

GREEN GODDESS BURGER & ROASTED POTATOES BOWL

HPP   SP   NSP

SERVES: 4
TIME: ABOUT 1 HOUR

Packed with loads of plant-based omega-3s, this is one of my favorite burger salads when I need a solid fix of green veggie goodness. Try it with *Super Hemp Protein Beet Burgers* (page 123), too!

1 Prepare the dressing, cover, and chill while preparing the rest of the ingredients. Make the burgers and keep warm or, if they have been prepared in advance, reheat on a griddle or wrap in foil and heat in the oven for about 10 minutes while you prepare the potatoes.

2 Roast the potatoes: Preheat the oven to 400°F. Line a baking sheet with parchment paper and lightly oil with olive oil. Dice the potatoes into ½-inch pieces and toss them on the sheet. Add the remaining ingredients for the potatoes and use tongs to combine everything together. Roast for 25 to 30 minutes, stirring occasionally, or until the potatoes are well browned and tender.

3 While the potatoes are cooking, clean and slice the salad vegetables if you haven't already.

4 Assemble the bowls: Line each bowl with the fresh veggies and top with a generous portion of roasted potatoes. Top with a burger. Serve immediately and pass around the dressing.

continued ➲

1 recipe *Cashew Hemp Goddess Dressing* (recipe follows)

4 *Green Goddess Burgers* (page 131)

ROASTED OLIVE ROSEMARY POTATOES

3 tablespoons olive oil, plus more for pan

2 pounds russet potatoes

1 cup kalamata olives, pits removed, roughly chopped

2 teaspoons salt

1 tablespoon dried rosemary, crumbled

1 teaspoon dried oregano

KALE SALAD

10 ounces baby kale leaves

1 cup thinly sliced radishes

4 scallions, thinly sliced

1 large red onion, thinly sliced

BURGER BOWLS

½ cup unroasted
cashew pieces

1 cup hot tap water

1 cup roughly chopped
fresh parsley

½ cup roughly chopped
fresh chives

2 garlic cloves

3 tablespoons
hemp seeds

1 tablespoon hemp oil
or omega-3 oil blend

2 tablespoons freshly
squeezed lemon juice

2 tablespoons white miso

Cashew Hemp Goddess Dressing

MAKES: ABOUT 2 CUPS DRESSING

A brisk, silky dressing of fresh herbs, white miso, and nutrient-dense hemp oil: or in place of hemp oil, use an omega-3 oil blend (such as Udo's). Serve with any bowl in this book or, naturally, with the *Green Goddess & Roasted Potato Bowl* (page 147).

1 In a blender, combine the cashew pieces and warm water. Cover and set aside for 15 to 20 minutes to soften.

2 Add the remaining ingredients and blend until as smooth and silky as possible. Taste and add a little extra miso or lemon juice, as desired. Serve, or for best flavor, cover and refrigerate for an hour. The dressing will thicken as it sets, just give it a good stir before serving. Eat within 3 days . . . after that, nice knowing you.

DILL PICKLE THOUSAND ISLAND CASHEW DRESSING

Pulse in 3 tablespoons of natural tomato ketchup.

Replace the parsley with fresh dill.

After it's blended, stir in ½ cup of finely chopped dill pickle.

CREAMY CUCUMBER GARLIC DRESSING

Increase the garlic to four cloves, find out which of your friends is secretly a vampire

Grate ½ pound of cucumber. Squeeze the cucumber shreds to remove as much water as possible, then stir into the dressing.

KORMA BURGER WITH COCONUT QUINOA & SPINACH SALAD

SERVES: 4
TIME: ABOUT 1 HOUR

Indian spices and coconut make everything taste more delicious. That's why I sprinkle cilantro chutney on my deep-fried Oreos. Okay, maybe not, even if I ate deep-fried Oreos. But this cardamom-flecked quinoa, lightly curried vinaigrette, and a hearty *Vegetable Korma Tofu Patty* (page 133) can turn any salad irresistible. And with the right time management, you can make this dish in no time: While the burgers bake, start the quinoa. Toward the end of the quinoa's cook time, prepare the dressing and wash and chop the veggies. Who knows, you may even still have time to fry up Oreos for dessert.

1 Make the burgers and keep warm or, if they have been prepared in advance, reheat on a griddle or wrap in foil and heat in the oven for about 10 minutes while you prepare the quinoa.

2 Start the quinoa: In a large saucepan, heat the drained quinoa over medium-high heat and toast for about 5 minutes, until dry and fragrant. Add the water, coconut milk, salt, and cardamom pods. Bring to a rapid boil, stir, lower the heat to low, and cover. Cook for about 20 minutes, or until liquid is absorbed and the quinoa is tender. Fluff with a fork and keep partially covered until ready to serve.

continued

4 *Vegetable Korma Tofu Patties* (page 133) (or more for really hungry people)

COCONUT QUINOA

1 cup uncooked quinoa, rinsed and drained

1 cup water

½ cup coconut milk

½ teaspoon salt

3 cardamom pods, gently crushed, or ¼ teaspoon ground cardamom

CURRY LIME VINAIGRETTE

2 tablespoons freshly squeezed lime juice

1 tablespoon olive oil

1 tablespoon pure maple syrup

1 teaspoon grated fresh ginger

½ teaspoon curry powder

½ teaspoon salt

(continued)

BURGER BOWLS

SPINACH SALAD

1 pound baby spinach, washed and spun dry

1 pint cherry tomatoes, sliced in half

1 red onion, sliced into half-moons

3 While the quinoa is cooking, in a glass measuring cup, whisk together the dressing ingredients.

4 Assemble the bowls: Scoop a generous portion of quinoa into a wide serving bowl. Top with the salad veggies, then add the burger. Serve immediately and pass around the dressing.

SUNNY OAT BURGER BOWL

SERVES: 4
TIME: ABOUT 1 HOUR

Chewy and flavorful Sunny Oat Burgers break free of an overtly hippie stereotype when paired with citrusy tahini dressing and roasted potatoes bathed in a Moroccan-inspired harissa marinade. Any hearty mix of greens is great here, but the sliced oranges and olives complete this unexpected bowl.

1 Preheat the oven to 400°F. Make the burgers and keep warm or, if they have been prepared in advance, reheat on a griddle or wrap in foil and heat in the oven for about 10 minutes while you prepare the potatoes.

2 Line a baking sheet with parchment paper and lightly oil with olive oil. Dice the potatoes into bite-size pieces and toss them on the sheet. Pulse together the remaining marinade ingredients, pour over the potatoes, and use tongs to toss the potatoes until coated in the marinade. Roast for 25 to 30 minutes, stirring occasionally, or until the potatoes are well browned and tender.

3 While the potatoes are roasting, blend the dressing ingredients together until smooth. Set aside while washing and slicing the salad ingredients.

continued ⮕

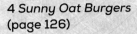

4 *Sunny Oat Burgers* (page 126)

HARISSA ROASTED POTATOES

3 tablespoons olive oil, plus more for pan

2 pounds Yukon gold or red potatoes, well scrubbed

2 tablespoons fresh or frozen finely chopped red chile peppers

4 garlic cloves

1 teaspoon ground coriander

½ teaspoon ground cumin

1 teaspoon salt

LEMON DILL TAHINI DRESSING

½ cup smooth tahini paste

¾ cup warm tap water

3 tablespoons freshly squeezed lemon juice

2 garlic cloves, peeled

1 cup fresh dill

½ teaspoon salt

(continued)

SALAD

6 cups baby kale or baby spinach leaves

2 large, juicy navel oranges, peeled and thinly sliced

1 large red onion, peeled and thinly sliced

½ cup kalamata or oil-cured black olives, pitted and roughly chopped

4 Arrange the salad ingredients in large serving bowls or plates. Top each salad serving with hot roasted potatoes and a Sunny Oat Burger. Serve and pass around the dressing. If the dressing is very thick, thin it out with a tablespoon or two of warm water before serving.

PRO-TIP: *There are many ways to reheat a veggie burger, but the best is still gently searing it on a cast-iron pan over medium heat. Heat enough to get the interior hot and the exterior deeply toasted, flipping occasionally.*

PINTO BBQ BURGER BOWL WITH SUCCOTASH SAUTÉ & ROASTED RED PEPPER DRESSING

SERVES: 4
TIME: 1 HOUR

The full-on summertime experience in a bowl: hearty BBQ burger, a smoky roasted red pepper dressing, and crispy red cabbage, all on top of a crunchy corn and lima bean sauté.

1 Make the burgers and keep warm or, if they have been prepared in advance, reheat on a griddle or wrap in foil and heat in the oven for about 10 minutes while you prepare the dressing and succotash.

2 Blend the dressing ingredients together until smooth. Set the dressing to chill in the fridge while you prepare the rest of the bowl.

3 Make the corn and lima bean sauté: Sauté the onion in the olive oil in a large skillet over medium heat for 2 minutes. Stir in the corn and lima beans and sauté for another 4 to 5 minutes, or until the limas are tender and hot. Stir in the scallions, dill, and salt and sauté for another minute. Turn off the heat and season with the lemon juice.

continued ➲

4 Pinto BBQ Seitan Burgers (page 135)

ROASTED RED PEPPER DRESSING

1 (12-ounce) jar roasted red peppers

¼ cup roughly diced shallots

2 tablespoons olive oil

1 tablespoon balsamic vinegar

1 tablespoon pure maple syrup

1 teaspoon smoked sweet paprika

½ teaspoon freshly ground black pepper

½ teaspoon salt

(continued)

ROASTED CORN & LIMA BEAN DILLY SAUTÉ

1 tablespoon olive oil

1 large yellow onion, peeled and diced

1 (16-ounce) bag frozen roasted corn, or about 3 cups home-roasted corn kernels

1 (16-ounce) bag frozen lima beans

2 scallions, white and green parts thinly sliced

½ cup roughly chopped fresh dill

½ teaspoon salt

1 tablespoon freshly squeezed lemon juice

TO ASSEMBLE

2 cups thinly sliced red cabbage

4 About 5 minutes before serving time, heat the burgers.

5 Assemble the bowl: Arrange the corn and lima bean sauté in large serving bowls or plates. Top with the shredded cabbage and a hot Pinto BBQ Seitan Burger. Serve and pass around the dressing.

PRO-TIP: There are many ways to reheat a veggie burger, but the best is still gently searing it on a cast-iron pan over medium heat. Heat enough to get the interior hot and the exterior deeply toasted, flipping occasionally.

FALAFEL BOWL WITH LEMON ROASTED POTATOES, BASIL LEMON CASHEW DRESSING, & CHOPPED MEDITERRANEAN SALAD

SERVES: 4
TIME: 1 HOUR

A beautiful bowl of toothsome baked falafel nestled on tender lemony marinated potatoes alongside cool, succulent cucumber salad and drizzled with bright basil lemon cashew dressing. Serve with warm thick pita bread if you desire a little something extra to sop up the juices from the salad and the potatoes. Consider serving with your favorite chili sauce, too!

1 Make the falafel balls and keep warm or, if they have been prepared in advance, reheat on a griddle or wrap in foil and heat in the oven for about 10 minutes while you prepare the dressing and potatoes.

2 Make the dressing: Combine the warm water and cashews and set aside to soak for 20 minutes (but stay away from Tumblr; get to work on the potatoes while you're at it instead). After a brief soak, blend the cashews and water with the remaining dressing ingredients until smooth. Chill until ready to use.

continued ➲

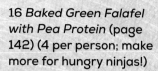

16 *Baked Green Falafel with Pea Protein (page 142)* (4 per person; make more for hungry ninjas!)

BASIL LEMON CASHEW DRESSING

¾ cup warm tap water

½ cup cashews

1 tablespoon olive oil

2 tablespoons freshly squeezed lemon juice

2 garlic cloves, peeled

1 cup lightly packed fresh basil leaves

½ teaspoon salt

LEMON DILL ROASTED POTATOES

½ cup vegan vegetable broth

¼ cup freshly squeezed lemon juice

¼ cup chopped fresh dill

4 garlic cloves, peeled and finely minced

2 teaspoons dried oregano, or 1 heaping tablespoon chopped fresh

1 teaspoon salt

2 pounds russet or other starchy potatoes, scrubbed

(continued)

3 Roast the potatoes: Preheat the oven to 400°F. In a 3-quart ceramic or glass baking dish, use a fork to whisk together the broth, lemon juice, garlic, oregano, and salt. Dice the potatoes (leave the skin on) into 1-inch pieces. Toss to coat in the marinade and cover the baking dish with foil. Seal the edges tight and bake for 20 minutes. Remove the foil, stir the potatoes, and bake, uncovered, for another 8 to 10 minutes, or until lightly browned but still a little bit saucy.

4 Make the salad: Combine all of the chopped veggies and the lemon juice in a bowl. Season with salt and pepper to taste.

5 Assemble the bowls: Scoop a generous portion of roasted potatoes into a wide serving bowl. Top with the chopped salad, then arrange a few falafel balls on top. Drizzle some dressing on top and pass around the remaining dressing.

CHOPPED SALAD

½ pound cucumbers, preferably Persian

1 pint cherry tomatoes, diced

1 cup chopped fresh parsley

1 large red onion, peeled and diced

Juice of 1 lemon

Salt and freshly ground black pepper

LENTIL WALNUT LOAF SUNDAY NIGHT ROAST BOWL

PPP   SP   LP

SERVES: 4
TIME: 1½ HOURS

4 big thick slices of *Lentil Walnut Loaf* (page 138)

ROSEMARY OLIVE ROASTED POTATOES

3 tablespoons olive oil, plus more for pan

2 pounds Yukon gold or red potatoes, well scrubbed

½ cup oil-cured black or kalamata olives, pitted

1 tablespoon dried rosemary, roughly chopped, or 2 tablespoons finely chopped fresh

1 teaspoon salt

MISO SHALLOT GRAVY

½ cup roughly chopped shallots

1 teaspoon dried thyme

1 tablespoon olive oil

2 tablespoons garbanzo bean flour

2 cups vegan vegetable broth

¼ cup miso, either white or red miso

Comfort food lightens up a little: Flash-sautéed garlicky collard greens are the foundation for hearty slices of extra-protein-worthy lentil loaf, rosemary roasted potatoes, and a simple miso gravy. And guess what? You can eat it any old day, not just Sunday.

1 Make the loaf and keep warm or, if it has been prepared in advance, reheat on a griddle or wrap in foil and heat in the oven for about 10 minutes while you prepare the potatoes.

2 Roast the potatoes: Preheat the oven to 400°F. Line a baking sheet with parchment paper and lightly oil with olive oil. Dice the potatoes into bite-size pieces and toss them on the sheet. Add the remaining ingredients for the potatoes and use tongs to combine everything together. Roast for 25 to 30 minutes, stirring occasionally, or until the potatoes are well browned and tender.

3 While the potatoes are roasting, prepare the gravy: In a large saucepan over medium heat, sauté together the shallots, thyme, and olive oil until the shallots are soft and tender, about 5 minutes. Stir in the garbanzo bean flour and fry until the flour is toasted, about 2 minutes. Pour in the vegetable broth in a steady stream and use a wire whisk to combine everything. Bring to an active simmer, stirring occasionally, for about 5 minutes, or until thickened. Ladle about ½ cup of thickened broth into a small bowl, add the miso, and use a fork to stir it into a smooth

paste. Lower the heat to low and whisk the miso mixture into the gravy. Stir to combine, turn off the heat, cover, and set the gravy aside until ready to serve.

4 Get those collards ready! Cut or tear away the main rib from the collard leaves, roll a few collards together into a tight cigar, and slice into ½-inch-wide ribbons. Wash and spin the collard ribbons dry.

5 Heat the olive oil in a wok over medium heat. Add half of the garlic, stir-fry for 30 seconds, then add half of the collards. Stir-fry the collards for 3 to 5 minutes, or until bright green, a little tender, but they still have a little bit of bite. Season to taste with salt, pepper, and a sprinkle of apple cider vinegar. Transfer the collards to half of the serving bowls or plates and repeat with the remaining collards.

6 Assemble the bowls: Top each serving of collards with a portion of roasted potatoes, a slice of loaf, and a healthy splash of gravy. Fill up the gravy boat (now you have an excuse) and pass it around the table while enjoying your bowls.

PRO-TIP: There are many ways to reheat a slice of veggie loaf, but the best is still gently searing it on a cast-iron pan over medium heat. Heat enough to get the interior hot and the exterior deeply toasted, flipping occasionally.

GARLICKY COLLARDS

- **2 pounds collard greens**
- **2 tablespoons olive oil**
- **6 garlic cloves, peeled and smashed**
- **Salt, pepper, and apple cider vinegar**

BLACK BEAN HEMP BURGER BOWL WITH REFRIED CORN QUINOA & MANGO CHIA SALSA

SERVES: 4
TIME: 1 HOUR

The burgers and the salsa are delicious, don't get me wrong, but what makes this bowl a stand-up-and-take-notice dish is the refried corn quinoa. You know you want to repeat it: Refried. Corn. Quinoa. Now stop talking and get cooking.

1 Make the burgers and keep warm or, if they have been prepared in advance, reheat on a griddle or wrap in foil and heat in the oven for about 10 minutes while you prepare the potatoes.

2 Make the salsa: Combine all the salsa ingredients in a glass bowl and cover. Set aside while preparing the rest of the meal; the chia seeds will plump up and the flavors will meld.

4 *Black Bean Hemp Burgers* (page 129) or, for something different, try with *Super Hemp Protein Beet Burgers* (page 123)

MANGO CHIA SALSA

2 ripe mangoes, diced into ½-inch pieces

½ cup lightly packed fresh cilantro leaves

1 small red onion, peeled and chopped

2 tablespoons freshly squeezed lime juice

1 tablespoon chia seeds

1 tablespoon olive oil

½ teaspoon salt

3 While the burgers are baking or heating, start the quinoa: Heat the olive oil in a large skillet or wok over medium-high heat. Add the scallions and corn and stir-fry together for 2 minutes. Add the diced red bell pepper and fry for another 2 minutes. Stir in the quinoa and fry for another 2 to 3 minutes, or until the quinoa is hot, then fold in the lime juice, paprika, cumin, and salt. Stir for another minute until hot and the quinoa is seasoned, then fold in the cilantro and remove from the heat.

4 Assemble the bowls: Scoop a generous portion of quinoa into a wide serving bowl. Top with a hot burger and a dollop of mango salsa, and garnish with avocado, tomato, and a handful of cabbage. Serve right away with any additional salsa.

REFRIED CORN QUINOA

2 tablespoons olive oil

2 scallions, thinly sliced

1 cup frozen roasted corn kernels

1 red bell pepper, seeded and diced

3 cups cooked white or red quinoa (about 1 cup uncooked; see page 15), chilled

2 tablespoons freshly squeezed lime juice

1 teaspoon smoked paprika

½ teaspoon ground cumin

½ teaspoon salt

½ cup roughly chopped fresh cilantro

TO ASSEMBLE

Sliced ripe avocado

Diced ripe tomato

Thinly sliced ribbons of red cabbage

4 Taco Salad Tortilla Bowls (recipe follows), or 1 cup large, restaurant-style tortilla chips per serving

KIMCHI SPICE TOFU

1 pound extra-firm tofu, pressed and drained (see pro-tip, page 114)

1 tablespoon olive oil

3 tablespoons vegan kimchi juice (see pro-tip)

4 garlic cloves, minced

1 teaspoon Korean red pepper powder

1 tablespoon freshly squeezed lime juice

1 tablespoon pure maple syrup or agave nectar

Big pinch of salt

SPINACH SALAD

2 tablespoons brown rice vinegar

2 tablespoons olive oil

1 tablespoon pure maple syrup or agave nectar

2 teaspoons toasted sesame oil

(continued)

KOREAN TOFU TACO SALAD

MAKES: 4 SALAD BOWLS
TIME: ABOUT 45 MINUTES

The way I see it, the Korean fusion taco transcended from food truck novelty to new classic. It was never meant to be just a flashy trend, because—let's face it—the flavors work. In this recipe, we take that saliva-inducing kimchi/Mexican portable bite and turn it into a beautiful and full-fledged dish. As a salad bowl, it has the benefits of a satisfying meal with the healthy rewards of more greens and protein. And that, my friend, is a win-win. Just like the Korean fusion taco.

1 If using tortilla bowls, prepare now and store in the oven (turn off the oven and open slightly to cool).

2 Prepare the kimchi tofu: Dice the pressed tofu into ½-inch chunks. Heat the olive oil over medium heat in a wok, add the tofu, and fry, stirring the tofu on occasion to evenly brown all the sides, 5 to 7 minutes. Whisk together the kimchi juice, garlic, Korean pepper powder, lime juice, maple syrup, and salt. Pour over the tofu and simmer, stirring occasionally, until the liquid has been absorbed. Remove from the heat and cover to keep warm while preparing the rest of the salad.

continued

> **PRO-TIP:** *If you can't find Korean red pepper powder, the closest substitute is a blend of half cayenne powder, half ancho chile powder. But do try and find the real deal if you have a good-size Asian market near you.*

SPINACH SALAD
(continued)

¼ teaspoon salt

1 cup cooked black beans, drained

1 cup diced ripe tomatoes

2 cups shredded romaine lettuce

2 cups baby spinach leaves, washed and spun dry

2 large scallions, green part only, thinly sliced

TO ASSEMBLE

1 cup vegan cabbage kimchi, squeezed and roughly chopped (see pro-tip)

1 large ripe avocado, thinly sliced

½ cup thinly sliced radishes

4 cilantro sprigs

4 teaspoons black sesame seeds

3 Ready the salad! In a cup, use a fork to whisk together the rice vinegar, olive oil, maple syrup, toasted sesame oil, and salt. In a large mixing bowl, combine the black beans, diced tomatoes, romaine lettuce, spinach, and scallions. Pour the dressing over the salad and use salad tongs to toss everything together.

4 Assemble the salad! Pile the dressed salad greens into the tortilla bowls, or if using tortilla chips, warm the chips slightly and pile into large serving bowls. Divide the tofu among the bowls and arrange the kimchi, avocado, radish, and a cilantro spring on top of each bowl. Sprinkle each bowl with black sesame seeds. Eat immediately, perhaps with an extra side of kimchi.

PRO-TIP: *Your average kimchi usually contains anchovies or fish sauce, making it not vegan at all. Always read those ingredient labels, even when the vegan police are not looking. And once you've got your fish-free kimchee in hand: Cabbage kimchi is typically very juicy, so it may be a matter of just spooning some directly out of the jar. If your kimchi is "young," you'll have to squeeze it a little to extract juice for the marinade . . . considering you already must for the rest of the salad, make sure to squeeze the kimchi over a bowl to collect the juices.*

Taco Salad Tortilla Bowls

Wheat tortillas bake in minutes into crispy tortilla bowls. For the best bowls, use the biggest tortillas you can find. If 10-inch are not available, layering two smaller tortillas together can form a big enough bowl to hold all those crazy salad ingredients.

1 Preheat the oven to 400°F. Arrange four 6-inch wide ovenproof bowls on a cookie sheet. Warm the tortillas (either in a microwave, or a hot pan or directly on a gas burner, holding with metal tongs) until soft and floppy. Press the tortillas into the bowls, crimping the sides to press into a bowl shape. Spray the insides with a touch of oil.

2 Bake the bowls for 8 to 10 minutes, or until crisp and golden brown; watch carefully so as not to burn. Remove from the oven and consume warm for the best flavor and texture.

TACO SALAD TORTILLA BOWLS

4 (10-inch) whole wheat or gluten-free flour tortillas

Olive oil cooking spray

GRAIN *and* NOODLE BOWLS

One chapter about the juxtaposition of warm and cool, crispy and creamy, fresh and comforting all nestled together in a bowl wasn't enough! I give you my ode to the perfection that is the fine gently convex surface.

Instead of burgers, the building block here is pasta, grains, or best of all, biscuits! Layered with veggies, fresh greens, and a savory protein, it's then all about the sauce.

Admittedly, preparing the elements of bowls sometimes can feel as if you're cooking a four-course meal. Each element requires a degree of care and respect; every bowl is the sum of a few tasty parts. My advice is to make half of the elements in advance: Sauces and baked goods can last for days (or weeks frozen), though proteins and fresh veggies are best done on the fly. Make the first two items (double or triple the recipe) on a Sunday night, enjoy bowls throughout the week, and become a true bowl Zen master.

TOMATO GRAVY & BISCUIT KALE BOWL

BRP **SP** **LP**

SERVES: 4
TIME: 45 MINUTES (NOT INCLUDING MAKING BISCUITS)

"Tomato gravy?" you say. "Is it good?" you ask. "Why tomato gravy instead of a bean gravy?" you wonder. You sure do ask a lot of nosy questions. Let me answer with my own inquiry: Why have a BLT sandwich when you could have this tasty pile of fluffy biscuits and tender kale, smothered in tangy, smoky tomato gravy? Trust me on this.

1 Make the gravy! Heat the olive oil in a large saucepan over medium heat. Add the onion and garlic and fry for 2 minutes, then stir in the thyme and garbanzo bean flour and fry for another 2 to 3 minutes, or until the flour is toasted golden brown.

2 Stir in the tomatoes, chickpeas, broth, paprika, and salt. Use an immersion blender to pulse the mixture until silky smooth. Cook, stirring occasionally, for 8 to 10 minutes, or until the gravy is thickened and hot. Season with pepper to taste. Remove from the heat and cover to keep warm.

3 Prepare the kale and tomatoes next: Remove the thick stems from the kale, stack and roll a few leaves at a time, and slice into thin shreds. Wash and spin dry the kale. Transfer to a mixing bowl and add the olive oil, vinegar, maple syrup, salt, and pepper. Use your hands to massage the oil and vinegar into the kale for a few minutes to soften the kale. Toss in the diced tomatoes.

continued ⮑

SMOKY TOMATO CHICKPEA GRAVY

2 tablespoons extra-virgin olive oil

1 cup diced yellow onion

3 garlic cloves, peeled and chopped

½ teaspoon dried thyme

2 tablespoons garbanzo bean flour

1 (16-ounce) can fire-roasted diced tomatoes (do not drain)

1 cup cooked chickpeas, drained and rinsed

1 cup richly flavored vegan vegetable broth

1 tablespoon smoked sweet paprika

½ teaspoon smoked or sea salt

Freshly ground black pepper

(continued)

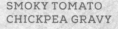

GRAIN + NOODLE BOWLS

4 Assemble that bowl! Split each biscuit and toast either on a preheated griddle or in a toaster oven. On each serving plate, make a mound of kale and top with a split biscuit. Ladle the gravy over everything, flourish with another twist of pepper, and serve immediately with the remaining hot gravy.

PRO-TIP: *"How can I add some bacon flavor?" you ask. Top each with either a few strips of* Tempeh Bacon Strips *(page 55) or a generous sprinkle of* My Best Coconut Bacon *(page 18) right before serving.*

KALE & TOMATOES

1 pound kale (lacitano kale is my favorite here)

1 tablespoon olive oil

1 tablespoon apple cider vinegar

1 teaspoon pure maple syrup

½ teaspoon salt

Few twists of freshly ground black pepper

1 pound ripe tomatoes, seeded and diced, or 1 pint cherry tomatoes, sliced in half

4 Fluffy Rice Protein Drop Biscuits (page 75)

GRAIN + NOODLE BOWLS

WHITE BEANS & MASHED POTATOES

1½ pounds small red or yellow waxy potatoes

1 (14-ounce) can white beans (large beans, such as butter or cannellini, are best), drained and rinsed

2 tablespoons olive oil

3 garlic cloves, minced

1 tablespoon dried rosemary

2 tablespoons freshly squeezed lemon juice

1 teaspoon salt

Plenty of freshly ground black pepper

(continued)

SEITAN MUSHROOM CHOPS WITH WHITE BEAN SMASHED POTATOES

SERVES: 4 HUNGRY NINJAS
TIME: 1½ HOURS

Even though it's 2016 or 2018 or 2025 (when you read this . . . I'm writing this on a hot 2015 summer day), I still occasionally feel the need to prove that vegan food can be as filling and badass as any omnivorous meal. This is a plant-based protein-delivery method bursting with umami flavors—mushrooms, seitan, beans—balanced by the bright crunch of a gently massaged Brussels sprouts salad and a touch of capers. The homemade seitan in this book was practically made for this recipe, but you can get right to it with any store-bought seitan your protein-craving heart desires; for best results, choose seitan that comes in long strips rather than chopped into small bits.

As this is a multicomponent meal, you'll start the recipes that either take longer to cook or can comfortably sit around a bit while the seitan, which should be served hot and saucy, is put together last.

1 Start the beans and potatoes: Scrub the potatoes and don't peel. If your potatoes are larger than about 1½ inches in diameter, cut in half. Transfer to a large pot, cover with about 3 inches of cold water, and bring to a rolling boil over high heat. Lower the heat to medium and simmer for about 20 minutes, or until the potatoes are tender enough to pierce with a fork but not falling-apart mushy. Drain, rinse with a little cold water, and set aside for a few minutes to cool slightly.

continued

MASSAGED BRUSSELS SPROUTS

1½ pounds Brussels sprouts

2 tablespoons red wine vinegar

2 tablespoons finely chopped shallots

1 tablespoon olive oil

½ teaspoon salt

Several generous twists of freshly ground black pepper

(continued)

2 While the potatoes are boiling, preheat the oven to 400°F. Cover a large baking sheet with parchment paper. Spread the slightly cooled potatoes on the paper, then use something wide and flat (such as the bottom of a small saucepan) to crush each potato chunk. Pour the beans, olive oil, garlic, lemon juice, rosemary, and salt over the potatoes and toss everything together to coat in the oil. Spread into a single layer and roast, stirring occasionally, for 20 to 25 minutes, or until the potatoes are roasted and the skins of the beans begin to split. Turn off the heat and cover loosely with foil to keep warm and moist.

3 Make the Brussels sprouts: While the potatoes are roasting, either use a knife (I vastly prefer this for larger, more appealing-looking shreds) or a food processor to shred the Brussels sprouts. Toss the shredded sprouts into a mixing bowl, add the remaining dressing ingredients, and use your hand to lightly massage the oil and vinegar into the sprouts until they are tender and glossy, about 2 minutes. Set aside.

4 Make the seitan chops: In a glass measuring cup, whisk together the vegetable broth, mustard, capers, and arrowroot. Slice the seitan on an angle into medallions about ½ inch thick. Heat half of the olive oil in a large skillet over medium-high heat, add half of the chopped shallots, and sauté for 2 to 3 minutes, or until the shallots are soft. Add half of the seitan and fry, flipping each piece occasionally, until hot, about 3 minutes. Pour half of the wine over the seitan to deglaze the pan and simmer for 2 minutes. Stir in half the mushrooms and sweat them for about

3 minutes, or until slightly softened and darkened. Pour half of the broth mixture over the seitan and mushrooms, and toss in half of the thyme. Simmer for 2 minutes, stirring occasionally, until hot and some of the liquid (but not all) has reduced and thickened. Twist on some freshly ground black pepper. Transfer the seitan to a ceramic dish, cover with foil, and repeat with the remaining seitan.

5 To serve, spread a portion of the beans and potatoes in each serving bowl and top with the seitan mixture. Nestle a portion of the Brussels sprouts salad in one corner and serve immediately!

SEITAN CHOPS

1¼ cups vegan vegetable broth

2 tablespoons vegan Dijon mustard

2 tablespoons capers

1 teaspoon arrowroot powder

½ recipe *The Steamed Seitan to Rule Them All* (page 16), or 10 ounces seitan

2 tablespoons olive oil

½ cup roughly chopped shallots

½ cup vegan red wine or more vegan vegetable broth

3 cups thickly sliced cremini or shiitake mushroom tops

4 large thyme sprigs, or 1 teaspoon dried

Several generous twists of freshly ground black pepper

FIVE-SPICE CHICKPEA PEANUT NOODLE BOWL

GF   LP

SERVES: 3-4
TIME: 1 HOUR

Sneaking chickpeas into an Asian dish? What am I thinking? I'm thinking roasted chickpeas rolled in fragrant five-spice powder, then covered in spicy thick peanut sauce on some noodles. And crunchy napa cabbage and radish salad as a vehicle for the sauce, I mean to get your daily dose of veggies covered.

1 Roast the chickpeas: Preheat the oven to 400°F and line a baking sheet with parchment paper. Spread the chickpeas on the prepared pan, sprinkle with the remaining chickpea ingredients, and toss around to coat with the sauce. Spread again in a single layer and roast for 20 to 25 minutes, stirring occasionally. The chickpeas should look roasty and slightly split.

2 Make the peanut sauce: In a mixing bowl, whisk together all the peanut sauce ingredients until smooth. Taste and season with more salt or vinegar, or thin out with more hot water or black tea, as desired.

continued ➲

ROASTED FIVE-SPICE CHICKPEAS

1 (15-ounce) can chickpeas, drained and rinsed

2 tablespoons tamari

1 tablespoons peanut oil

2 teaspoons Chinese five-spice powder

SPICY PEANUT SAUCE

½ cup peanut butter

⅓ cup warm tap water or hot brewed black tea

1 tablespoon sriracha or any garlicky Asian chile sauce

1 tablespoon rice vinegar

1 tablespoon coconut sugar or organic brown sugar

2 garlic cloves, peeled

1 (1-inch cube) peeled fresh ginger

1 teaspoon toasted sesame oil

¼ teaspoon salt, or to taste

(continued)

GRAIN + NOODLE BOWLS

NOODLES & SALAD

4 to 6 ounces uncooked rice noodles (for gluten free version), udon, or noodles

2 teaspoons toasted sesame oil

½ pound finely chopped napa cabbage

1 bunch scallions, thinly sliced

1 cup thinly sliced radishes or shredded daikon

A few handfuls of arugula, baby spinach, or other favorite bittersweet salad greens

3 Make the noodles: Cook the noodles according to the package directions, rinse with a little bit of cold water (not enough to completely chill the noodles, just enough to make them slippery), toss with the toasted sesame oil, and distribute evenly among the serving bowls. Top each bowl with equal portions of the salad veggies, then the chickpeas, and last, drizzle with some peanut sauce. Serve with any remaining peanut sauce on the side.

LEMONGRASS TEMPEH MEATBALLS WITH PEANUT SATAY SAUCE

SERVES: 3-4
TIME: 1½ HOURS

You think that after nearly a decade of writing vegan cookbooks, I would get over the weirdness of calling something a "meatball." Then again, "toothsome Vietnamese-inspired spheres nestled in peanut sauce" is a mouthful. And what a mouthful: Served on a bed of rice vermicelli with steamed bok choy, sprigs of fresh cilantro and mint, and a generous sprinkle of peanuts, these meatballs, tempehballs, whatever you want to call them, are just freakin' delicious. And if balls isn't your thing at ALL (I don't ask), you're invited to shape the mixture into little patties, as shown in the stunning recipe photograph.

1 Make the tempeh balls: Dice the tempeh into 1-inch cubes. In a small saucepan, cover the tempeh with 2 inches of cold water and bring to a boil. Lower the heat to low, partially cover, and simmer the tempeh for 5 minutes, or until soft. Drain and transfer to a large mixing bowl.

2 Add the remaining meatball ingredients, except the olive oil. Thoroughly mash everything to form a thick, chunky mixture. Taste and season with more salt, if desired. Divide the mixture into fourteen balls (about 1 heaping tablespoon each), and gently roll and press into balls.

continued ➲

LEMONGRASS TEMPEH BALLS

1 (8-ounce) package tempeh

1 cup cooked adzuki beans

3 tablespoons tamari

¼ cup finely chopped shallots

½ cup roughly chopped fresh cilantro

1 tablespoon prepared lemongrass or finely minced fresh

1 teaspoon grated fresh ginger

2 garlic cloves, peeled and minced

½ cup panko bread crumbs

Olive oil, for frying

(continued)

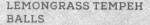

GRAIN + NOODLE BOWLS

PEANUT SATAY SAUCE

½ cup peanut butter

⅓ cup Thai full-fat canned coconut milk

¼ cup warm tap water

1 tablespoon sriracha or any garlicky Asian chile sauce

2 tablespoons freshly squeezed lime juice

2 tablespoons tamari

2 tablespoons minced shallots

1 teaspoon grated fresh ginger

NOODLES & GARNISHES

1 (8-ounce) package rice noodles

1 pound baby bok choy, cleaned

1 bunch fresh cilantro

Handful each of fresh mint leaves

Handful of fresh Thai basil leaves

Julienned carrot or daikon

Asian chile garlic sauce, hoisin sauce, or soy sauce, as desired

3 Slick the bottom of a cast-iron skillet with olive oil and heat over medium heat. Fry half of the balls, carefully turning the balls around until all the sides are golden brown. Transfer the balls to a dish and repeat with the remaining balls. Cover and keep warm while preparing the sauce and noodles.

4 Make the peanut sauce: In a blender or food processor, blend all the peanut sauce ingredients until smooth. The sauce will thicken slightly as it cools, so right before serving, taste and thin with more coconut milk, or add more lime juice or salt, if desired.

5 Make the noodles: Prepare the rice noodles according to the package directions, and rinse with warm water to prevent sticking. Steam the baby bok choy just long enough to make it bright green, but be careful not to overcook. Arrange the noodles in bowls and top with the tempeh meatballs and bok choy. Drizzle the peanut sauce on top and scatter the tops of the bowls with the cilantro, mint, Thai basil, and carrot/daikon. Serve right away with the extra peanut sauce and your choice of (or all of them) Asian chili garlic sauce, hoisin sauce, or soy sauce, on the side.

PRO MAC WITH ROASTED BROC

SERVES: 4-6
TIME: ABOUT 1½ HOURS

No, this isn't a recipe to build a Mac Pro, but this casserole is equally well engineered. The butternut puree adds depth and richness and helps hydrate the pea protein; the bread crumb topping adds grainy texture; the complementary side of roasted broccoli made as the mac bakes will simply make your mom happy. This recipe might require some extra computing power, but I know you can do it. To speed things up, make your oven do double duty: Bake the casserole on the bottom rack while roasting the broccoli on the top rack.

1 Cover the cashews with 2 inches of hot water and soak for about 20 minutes, until softened. Drain and discard the water.

2 Cook the pasta according to the package directions, BUT slightly undercook by 2 to 3 minutes so the pasta is very firm. Drain and rinse with plenty of cold water in a colander. Set over a sink to drain while preparing the rest of the recipe.

3 Preheat the oven to 400°F and generously oil a 7 x 11 x 2-inch baking dish. Also, line a large baking sheet with parchment paper. In a blender, puree the drained cashews, vegetable broth, butternut puree, pea protein powder, nutritional yeast, mustard, garlic powder, turmeric, and salt.

continued ⮑

¾ cup unroasted cashew pieces

10 ounces high-protein pasta shells, spirals, or elbows, such as quinoa pasta or brown rice pasta (for gluten-free mac)

Olive oil, for baking dish

2 cups vegan vegetable broth

1 cup butternut squash puree (see pro-tip)

½ cup pea protein powder

3 heaping tablespoons nutritional yeast

1 tablespoon vegan Dijon mustard

2 teaspoons garlic powder

½ teaspoon ground turmeric

½ teaspoon salt

(continued)

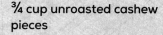

GRAIN + NOODLE BOWLS

BREAD CRUMB TOPPING

1¼ cups whole wheat or gluten-free bread crumbs

2 tablespoons nutritional yeast

2 tablespoons shelled hemp seeds

2 tablespoons olive oil

½ teaspoon salt

ROASTED BROCCOLI

4 cups broccoli florets

2 tablespoons olive oil

1 shallot, minced

½ teaspoon salt

Freshly squeezed lemon juice

Red pepper flakes

4 In bowl, toss together the bread crumb topping ingredients, rubbing the crumbs together with your fingers to distribute the olive oil evenly. Sprinkle about a quarter of the crumbs onto the bottom of the baking dish.

5 In another bowl, stir together the drained cooked pasta and cashew sauce. Pour into the prepared baking pan. Spread the crumbs in an even layer over the casserole. Cover the casserole tightly with foil.

6 On the baking sheet or in a mixing bowl, toss together the broccoli ingredients, rubbing the broccoli with your fingers to distribute the oil and spices evenly. Spread in an even layer on the prepared baking sheet.

7 Bake the mac casserole on the bottom rack of the oven for 20 minutes. After 20 minutes, remove the foil from the top of the casserole and also slide the broccoli pan onto the top rack. Occasionally stir the broccoli as it roasts.

8 Roast the broccoli for 20 minutes, or until tender and the tips are lightly browned. The casserole should be ready in about 15 minutes, or when the crumb topping is golden.

PRO-TIP: *For this recipe, I prefer to steam peeled 1-inch chunks of butternut squash for 20 to 25 minutes until very tender. Once it's done, puree it with an immersion blender or mash like crazy until very smooth. But really what I actually prefer most busy days is to buy frozen butternut puree (you can even find it organic!), thaw according to the package directions, and use that in this recipe for some seriously ridiculous convenience.*

CREAMY TOMATO TOFU CURRY WITH CILANTRO GARBANZO FLATBREAD

SP   LP

SERVES: 4
TIME: ABOUT 1½ HOURS

A sneaky twist on the always crowd-pleasing, slightly sweet, creamy, tomato-based vegetable curries: In place of coconut milk, a puree of white beans and tomato not only boosts the protein (and fiber) count alongside pressed, seared tofu, but adds a deep, creamy richness. Serve with basmati rice or *Cilantro Mint Garbanzo Bean Flatbreads* (page 84).

1 Start the tofu: Drain and then press the tofu according to the pro-tip on page 114.

2 Meanwhile, blend together the curry paste ingredients in a food processor or blender.

3 While the tofu is pressing, chop the vegetables for the broth: Peel and slice the onion into thick half-moons. Remove the root and green part of the leek, slice in half, wash well to remove any grit, and chop into ½-inch-thick pieces. Chop the cauliflower and squash into bite-size pieces, and the green beans into bite-size lengths. This should keep you plenty busy while that tofu presses, but when it's ready to go, dice the tofu into ½-inch cubes.

4 Heat 1 tablespoon of the coconut oil in a large wok over medium-high heat. Brown the tofu for 6 to 8 minutes, stirring occasionally and always spreading out in one layer for even browning. Transfer the tofu to a plate.

continued ➲

TOFU & VEGETABLES

1 pound firm tofu

2 tablespoons coconut oil

1 leek

3 cups cauliflower florets

2 cups zucchini or yellow summer squash

1 cup green beans

1 large yellow onion

CURRY PASTE

½ cup minced shallots

2 garlic cloves, peeled

1 tablespoon minced fresh ginger

1 to 3 fresh red chiles

2 Medjool dates, pitted

1 tablespoon mild curry powder

1 tablespoon freshly squeezed lemon juice

½ teaspoon ground turmeric

1 teaspoon salt

(continued)

GRAIN + NOODLE BOWLS

TOMATO WHITE BEAN PUREE

1 (14-ounce can) fire-roasted tomatoes (do not drain)

1 (14-ounce can) white beans, drained and rinsed

1½ cups water

1 cup frozen green peas

1 cup chopped fresh cilantro

5 Heat the remaining coconut oil and fry the onion and leek until just starting to soften, about 5 minutes. Stir in the curry paste and fry for 2 minutes, stirring constantly. Add the cauliflower, squash, and green beans and fry for another 2 minutes.

6 Make the tomato white bean puree: In a blender, puree the diced tomatoes, white beans, and water. Stir into the wok mixture and simmer the curry for another 15 minutes or so, or until the vegetables are tender but not mushy and the curry has thickened up a little. Taste the sauce and adjust the seasoning with more salt or lemon juice, if desired. Stir in the frozen peas and cilantro, simmer for 1 minute, and remove from the heat.

7 The curry will be crazy hot! If possible, set it aside to cool for a few minutes before serving with hot rice or bread.

continued

Cilantro Mint Garbanzo Bean Flatbreads (page 84)

WINTER VEGETABLE CURRY

Curries are endlessly flexible when it comes to whatever vegetable you want to toss into the mix. The main recipe should use tender, faster-cooking summer produce. If you have potatoes and pumpkin on hand, it's easy enough to transform this into a substantial, hearty winter stew.

Here are my suggested adjustments for a winter curry:

✖ Replace the cauliflower with diced waxy potatoes OR use half potato, half cauliflower.

✦ Replace the summer squash with diced pumpkin, butternut, or whatever winter squash you like.

✖ Omit the green beans, but stir in 2 to 3 cups of chopped kale or spinach along with the green peas.

✖ Increase the water to 2½ cups, pureed with the tomatoes and beans

MOST important, this curry will need a longer cooking time to soften up the potatoes and winter squash. Maybe double the cooking time to 40 minutes. Watch carefully, and don't be afraid to stir in an additional ½ to 1 cup of water toward the end, if the curry looks too thick or in danger of burning. You may need to up the salt a bit, so taste toward the end and season with more salt and lemon juice, as needed.

WAFFLED TOFU, WAFFLES & COLLARDS BOWL WITH SPICY MAPLE SYRUP

SERVES: 4
TIME: 1½ HOURS

Waffles. Bowls. Together at last. But not just any waffles: This ninja gives you waffled tofu. Yes, that lovably adaptable soy patty meets the iron for a crisp, protein-laden vehicle. Did I even mention the sweet, savory delights of the orange-kissed collards and sriracha-laced maple syrup? I digress! ANYway, you're gonna want to waffle everything after this.

1 Prepare the waffles and keep warm (If you're making the waffles now, prepare the waffles first, then go directly to making the tofu [step 4]). Or make waffles in advance, then toast right before serving.

2 Begin the tofu: Drain and slice the tofu into eight equal slabs, then pat down the slices with a clean kitchen towel to remove some of the excess water. In a baking dish, whisk together the tamari, olive oil, maple syrup, paprika, and cumin. Marinate the tofu in this mixture for 20 minutes or up to 2 hours, flipping occasionally to absorb more marinade.

continued ➲

Enough *Wake Up Waffles* (page 48), for 4: either 4 Belgian-style or 8 square

WAFFLED TOFU

1 pound firm tofu

3 tablespoons tamari

2 tablespoons olive oil

1 tablespoon pure maple syrup

1 teaspoon smoked sweet paprika

½ teaspoon ground cumin

ZESTY ORANGE COLLARDS

2 pounds collards

2 tablespoons olive oil

2 garlic cloves, minced

½ cup freshly squeezed orange juice

½ teaspoon salt

Freshly ground black pepper

(continued)

SPICY MAPLE SYRUP

½ cup warmed pure maple syrup

1 to 2 tablespoons sriracha sauce, to taste

3 Meanwhile, make the collards: Remove the thick main stem from the collards. Roll up a few tightly, slice into ½-inch ribbons, then wash and spin dry. In a wok or large skillet, heat the olive oil over medium heat. Add the garlic and collards and stir-fry for 2 minutes, or until collards have softened and are bright green. Pour in the orange juice and salt and stir-fry for another 2 to 3 minutes, or until most of the liquid has been absorbed and the collards are tender but still green. Season with pepper, cover to keep warm, and set aside.

4 Prepare the waffled tofu! Preheat a waffle iron on HIGH according to the manufacturer's directions. Place one layer of tofu at a time in the iron and bake for 3 to 4 minutes, or until the tofu is browned and hot.

5 Make the syrup: Whisk together the maple syrup and sriracha.

6 Serve the waffles! Place a mound of collards in each plate or a wide, shallow serving bowl. Arrange the waffles on top: I like to slice the waffles in half or quarters, but it's up to you. Place two or three slices of waffled tofu on the waffles. Serve right away and pass around the maple syrup!

SPINACH & COCONUT BACON SALAD, SWEET POTATO BISCUITS, & BUTTON UP WHITE BEAN GRAVY

SERVES: 4
TIME: 1 HOUR

Because there are never too many reasons to eat coconut bacon. Add spinach and feel positively virtuous. While this bowl is indeed a mashup of a few recipes in this book, think of it as the super group you're actually happy the original bands broke up to create.

1 Prepare the biscuits up to a day in advance. You can do the same with the gravy, or make it while the biscuits bake. Whatever you end up doing, heat the gravy first and cover to keep it warm, then reheat the biscuits, preferably split and toasted on a dry griddle.

2 Make the salad: In a cup or small bowl, whisk together the red wine vinegar, olive oil, shallots, mustard, and salt. In a large bowl, toss the dressing with the spinach, apple, celery, and onion. Add half of the coconut bacon and toss a few times.

3 Assemble the bowls! Divide the salad among large, shallow serving bowls. Top with the hot, split biscuits and ladle the gravy on top. Sprinkle with the remaining coconut bacon and serve right away with a side of gravy and a twist of freshly ground black pepper.

8 *Sweet Potato Pea Biscuits* (page 79) (about 2 per serving)

Button Up White Bean Gravy (page 59)

SPINACH & COCONUT BACON SALAD

¼ cup red wine vinegar

3 tablespoons extra-virgin olive oil

2 tablespoons finely minced shallots

1 tablespoon vegan Dijon mustard

¼ teaspoon salt

1 pound baby spinach

1 firm, tart, red or green apple, cored and diced

1 large celery stalk, sliced very thinly on the bias (about ¼ inch or less)

1 large red onion, peeled, quartered, and thinly sliced

1 cup *My Best Coconut Bacon* (page 18)

Freshly ground black pepper

MODERN-DAY SEITAN MACRO BOWL

MAKES: 3–4 LARGE BOWLS
TIME: ABOUT 2½ HOURS, INCLUDING MAKING SEITAN

ADZUKI BEAN BROWN RICE

2 scallions, white and green parts divided and very thinly sliced

2 teaspoons toasted sesame oil

1 cup uncooked short-grain brown rice

1¾ cups water

½ teaspoon salt

1 (14-ounce) can or 1½ cups cooked adzuki beans, rinsed and drained

TAHINI-MISO DRESSING

½ cup sesame tahini

¼ cup white miso

⅔ cup warm tap water

GINGER SCALLION SEITAN

⅔ cup freshly squeezed orange juice

1 tablespoon finely minced fresh ginger

½ teaspoon salt

4 scallions, thinly sliced

(continued)

Brown rice. Vegetable. Bean. Protein. Rinse. Repeat. What seemingly all vegan food was until about a decade or two ago. You'd think we'd never be nostalgic for those little piles on a plate with a dash of soy sauce.

But there's a reason this combo endures: It's comforting, tasty, and annoyingly healthy. This is my slightly updated version: I cook the beans and rice together in a traditional Japanese-style blend of nutty sweet adzuki beans and brown rice. And then there's good old miso-tahini sauce. The orange-gingery seitan, easy enough to simmer on the stovetop in minutes, gives this a new spark. As for the veggies, go raw, cooked, or use a combo of both.

There are a few stages to this bowl—surprise! Don't spend all day in the kitchen: Make the seitan a week or more in advance, freeze, and thaw for an hour or two before dinner. The sauce and rice can be made the day before. The veggies and the marinade are easy enough to make it when you need it.

1 Make the rice: In a large saucepan over medium heat, fry the sliced white part of the scallions in the toasted sesame oil for a minute. Stir in the rice and fry for another minute, then add the water, salt, and beans. Turn up the heat and bring to a rolling boil for a minute. Lower the heat to low, cover, and simmer for 40 to 50 minutes, or until all the water has been absorbed by the rice and the rice is tender. Turn off the heat and cover to keep warm, or refrigerate and reheat when ready to assemble your bowls.

2 Make the miso-tahini dressing: In a mixing bowl, stir the tahini and miso together (a rubber spatula works best for combining these thick pastes) until smooth. Stream in the warm water and stir to create a smooth, thick sauce. If chilled, the sauce will thicken considerably, so it's okay to loosen it up with a little more warm water.

3 Make the seitan: In a large bowl, combine the orange juice, ginger, salt, and scallions. Add the seitan, toss in the marinade, and marinate for at least 10 minutes or overnight. In a large wok, heat the olive oil over medium heat. Lift the seitan out of the marinade and into the wok. Fry, flipping occasionally, for 3 to 5 minutes, or until the seitan is golden brown. Pour in the remaining marinade and simmer until most of it has been absorbed but the seitan is still juicy.

4 Make that bowl! In a large serving bowl, mound a large scoop of the warm rice. Arrange your choice of at least two veggies and the seitan on top, sprinkle with the sliced green scallions, and serve with the tahini-miso dressing on the side. I like to also sprinkle everything with arame seaweed flakes and umeboshi plum vinegar.

MODERN-DAY TOFU MACRO BOWL

Substitute 1 pound of firm tofu in place of the seitan. If desired, press the tofu prior to marinating. See the pro-tip on page 114.

PRO-TIP: Of course, you can use canned beans. I've been there. And the recipe notes 'em! However, homemade beans are always tastier. In the instance of adzuki beans, this is even truer: The firmness and superior flavor of home-simmered beans beats the tiny pants off of mushy canned adzuki beans.

GINGER SCALLION SEITAN (continued)

8 to 10 ounces store-bought seitan, thinly sliced OR ½ recipe *The Steamed Seitan to Rule Them All* (page 16), sliced into bite-size strips

2 tablespoons olive or canola oil

VEGETABLES & GARNISHES
(choose 2 or more)

3 cups finely shredded green or red cabbage

3 cups raw or lightly blanched broccoli or cauliflower florets

4 cups gently blanched baby bok choy

4 cups gently blanched, torn spinach or kale leaves

3 cups steamed, diced butternut squash

1½ cups raw or lightly steamed green peas

1 cup shredded raw daikon

Dried powdered arame seaweed

Umeboshi plum vinegar

BLACKEST BEAN CHOCOLATE SEITAN CHILI & CORN BREAD BOWL

SERVES: 4-6

TIME: ABOUT 2 HOURS, INCLUDING MAKING CHILI AND CORN BREAD AT THE SAME TIME

From the darkest depths of the abyss emerges this impish blackest of black bean seitan chili—the unholy coloration not just from the wheat meat with the diabolical-sounding name and black beans themselves, but from the addition of smoked paprika and dark cocoa powder. It's evil, and like most evil things, temptingly delicious. But be warned: When you stare into the chili, the chili stares back at you. Serve with corn bread and crunchy peanut cabbage slaw!

1 Make the chili: Heat a dry skillet over low heat and toast the slivered almonds for 2 to 3 minutes, or until they start to turn golden. Stir in the ancho chile powder, smoked paprika, oregano, cumin, cinnamon, and anise seeds. Stir and toast the spices for 1 minute, watching carefully so as not to burn. Transfer the nuts and spices to a spice grinder and grind until smooth. Or, if you prefer, pound the spices with a mortar and pestle to a gritty powder.

2 In a large soup pot, heat half of the olive oil over medium heat. Add the seitan and sauté for 5 minutes, or until the edges start to brown. Stir in the remaining oil, onion, and garlic and fry until soft, about 3 minutes. Add the tomatoes and simmer for 2 minutes, stirring occasionally to remove any bits of browned seitan stuck to the bottom of the pot.

continued ➲

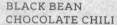

BLACK BEAN CHOCOLATE CHILI

¼ cup slivered almonds

1 tablespoon ancho chile powder

1 tablespoon smoked sweet paprika

1 tablespoon dried oregano

2 teaspoons ground cumin

1 teaspoon ground cinnamon

1 teaspoon anise or fennel seeds

3 tablespoons olive oil

10 ounces prepared seitan or homemade seitan, diced into 1-inch chunks

1 large yellow onion, peeled and diced

4 garlic cloves, peeled and chopped

1 (28-ounce) can fire-roasted diced tomatoes (do not drain)

2½ cups richly flavored vegan vegetable broth

(continued)

GRAIN + NOODLE BOWLS

BLACK BEAN CHOCOLATE CHILI (continued)

1 (16-ounce) can black beans, drained and rinsed

½ teaspoon salt

¼ cup vegan dark chocolate chips

PEANUT CABBAGE TOPPING

3 cups finely shredded red cabbage

¼ cup chopped fresh cilantro

2 tablespoons freshly squeezed lime juice

¼ cup finely ground salted roasted peanuts

Pinch of salt

1 big wedge or muffin of *Hempy Corn Bread* (page 77) per person

3 While chili is simmering, prepare the cabbage topping: Toss together all the topping ingredients in a mixing bowl and set aside until ready to serve.

4 To finish the chili, add the almond mixture, broth, beans, and salt. Lower the heat to low, partially cover, and simmer for 10 minutes, stirring occasionally. Stir in the chocolate chips until melted. Turn off the heat and cover the chili.

5 Toast the corn bread wedges on a lightly oiled skillet over medium-high heat, flipping occasionally, until hot and lightly browned. If using corn bread muffins, split in half horizontally, then toast.

6 Place one piece of toasted corn bread in each large, wide serving bowl. Ladle on the chili, then top with peanut cabbage topping and serve immediately.

PRO-TIP: *Both the corn bread and the chili can be made a day in advance and reheated.*

SWEET TREATS

Have you been eating your leafy green vegetables? Hitting the gym every day? Replying to every text message with thoughtfully selected, fully spelled-out words instead of that smiling puppy face and LOMAFOA? Then, you deserve a protein-packed sweet treat. Without delay, the reason you picked up this book: BROWNIES!

. . . and blondies and cookies and even wholesome portable sweet snacks with healthy hemp, brown rice, or pea protein. Even a fully loaded granola bar and a rice pudding to keep stocked in the fridge for necessary spoonfuls throughout the weekend.

I made these treats a little sweeter for the masses, but at home I prefer my treats to have a little less sugar (no matter what the source, organic sugar or maple syrup). Sound good to you? Then try cutting down the sugar in each recipe: ½ cup to ⅓ cup, ⅔ cup to ½ cup, and so on . . .

Protein-enriched desserts are easier to come by in many natural food markets, but really it's so much better to make them fresh in your kitchen. And so much tastier than anything you can buy, these sturdy cookies are bars that are easy to freeze. Get the hang of these recipes and you, too, will soon be switching out fruits, nuts, whole-grain flours, and even protein powders for never-ending variations.

BLACK BEAN HEMP BROWNIES

HPP   LP

MAKES: 12 BROWNIES
TIME: 45 MINUTES, NOT INCLUDING COOLING TIME

Finally, a hemp brownie that's legal to eat! Packed with protein (with the help of our friends, black beans) and fiber, these brownies will be a hit with both health-conscious snackers and straight-up chocoholics (I don't judge). Easy to make and even easier to eat, these brownies are so good, you won't even mind that they don't cause hallucinations.

Coconut oil, for pan

¼ cup plus 1 tablespoon Dutch-process cocoa powder

½ cup white whole wheat flour

½ cup hemp protein powder

1 teaspoon baking powder

¼ teaspoon salt

1 cup vegan chocolate chips

½ cup coconut oil, softened

1 cup cooked black beans, drained and rinsed

¼ cup hot tap water

½ cup organic dark brown sugar

½ cup organic sugar

1½ teaspoons pure vanilla extract

⅓ cup walnuts, chopped

1 Preheat the oven to 350°F. Generously grease an 8-inch square baking pan and dust it with 1 tablespoon of the cocoa, tapping out any excess.

2 In a large mixing bowl, whisk together the flour, hemp protein powder, remaining ¼ cup of cocoa powder, and the baking powder and salt. Form a well in the center.

3 Over a double boiler or in a microwave, melt half of the chocolate chips: if using a double boiler, melt over gently boiling water, stirring occasionally until smooth; if using a microwave, cook for 1 minute over high heat, stir the softened chips, then microwave another 30 seconds one or two more times, stirring chips until smooth and glossy. Stir in the coconut oil, melting it into the chocolate until smooth. In a food processor, blend the beans with hot water until the beans are totally smooth. Add the melted chocolate mixture and blend until smooth again. Add the sugars and vanilla and pulse until smooth. Pour the wet mixture into the well of the dry ingredients and mix with a rubber spatula only enough to just moisten the dry ingredients, then fold in the remaining chocolate chips and mix only enough to combine.

4 Use a rubber spatula to transfer all the batter to the prepared baking pan and spread in an even layer to the edges of the pan.

5 Sprinkle the top with the walnuts. Bake for 25 to 30 minutes, until the brownies are firm and the top looks dry. Let cool completely before cutting into twelve bars. Store in a loosely covered container; best enjoyed within 2 days of baking. Do I really need to remind you to eat brownies?

HAZELNUT CHIP NAVY BLONDIES

MAKES: 16 BLONDIES
TIME: 45 MINUTES, NOT INCLUDING COOLING TIME

Coconut oil, for pan

¾ cup plus 1 tablespoon unbleached all-purpose flour

⅓ cup pea protein powder

1 teaspoon baking powder

¼ teaspoon salt

1 cup cooked navy beans, drained and rinsed

⅓ cup canola oil or refined coconut oil

¼ cup hot water

⅔ cup organic dark brown sugar

½ cup organic sugar

2 teaspoons pure vanilla extract

¼ cup vegan chocolate chips, or 3 ounces vegan semisweet chocolate, roughly chopped

¼ cup chopped hazelnuts or walnuts

Packed with protein and fiber from pea protein and navy beans, these blondies—the coy, butterscotch-flavored cousin of the brownie—are the sweet treat that nine out of ten fitness instructors recommend, had I bothered to survey any. Surveys or not, wholesome vegan blondies are welcome everywhere!

1 Preheat the oven to 350°F. Line an 8-inch square pan with foil. Lightly oil the foil, add 1 tablespoon of the flour, and move the pan around, tapping the sides to coat the inside bottom and edges of the pan with flour.

2 In a large mixing bowl, stir together remaining ¾ cup of flour and the pea protein powder, baking powder, and salt.

3 In a food processor, blend the beans with the oil and hot water until completely smooth. Add the sugars and vanilla and pulse until smooth. Pour the wet mixture into the dry ingredients and with a rubber spatula fold together until slightly moistened, then add half of the chocolate chips and mix until just combined. The batter will be very thick, and that's okay. Don't overmix!

4 Scoop the batter into the prepared baking pan and use the rubber spatula to evenly spread the batter to the edges of the pan. Sprinkle the top with the remaining chocolate chips and the nuts. Bake for 20 minutes and let cool completely, then remove the blondies by picking up the edges of the foil. Slice into sixteen squares, store loosely covered, and eat them all or share them within about 2 days.

PEANUT BUTTER COCONUT CHERRY CHEWIES

GF

MAKES: 12 COOKIES
TIME: 30 MINUTES, NOT INCLUDING COOLING TIME

Sometimes the weight of the adult world (taxes, Sunday morning news shows, going to the dentist) is too much. That's why peanut butter cookies exist: to make you feel like a child. These dense and chewy protein cookies freeze well, so next time your day job's got you down but you still want protein like a grown-up, you know what to do.

1 Preheat the oven to 350°F and line a baking sheet with parchment paper.

2 Combine the topping ingredients in a small, shallow bowl.

3 Make the cookies: In a large bowl, mash together the banana, peanut butter, maple syrup, vanilla, and almond extract until smooth. Stir in the pea protein powder until smooth. Fold in the oats, salt, baking soda, and dried cherries. The dough will be sticky; that's okay!

4 Using an ice-cream dipper for the easiest scooping of the sticky dough, or lightly oiling your fingers to shape the dough, drop generous rounded tablespoons into the topping mixture. Roll to coat, then transfer to the prepared baking sheet, leaving 1 inch apart. Gently flatten each cookie to about 1 inch thick. Bake for 12 minutes, or until the bottoms are lightly browned. Let cool completely before storing loosely covered.

TOPPING

½ cup finely chopped roasted unsalted peanuts

½ cup grated unsweetened coconut

COOKIES

1 large ripe banana

⅓ cup smooth unsalted peanut butter

¼ cup pure maple syrup

½ teaspoon pure vanilla extract

½ teaspoon almond extract

⅓ cup pea protein powder

1 cup old-fashioned rolled oats

½ teaspoon salt

¼ teaspoon baking soda

¼ cup dried cherries or cranberries

DARK CHOCOLATE ALMOND CHEWIES

 GF   HPP   NSP

MAKES: 12 COOKIES
TIME: 30 MINUTES, NOT INCLUDING COOLING TIME

Deep cocoa flavor and rich chewy texture, loaded with good-for-you oats, banana, almonds, antioxidant-rich cocoa, and a hemp protein powder in these lovely lumps. Not too sweet, the ideal breakfast treat without the sugary crash later, perfect with black coffee.

TOPPING

2 tablespoons cacao nibs

½ cup finely chopped almonds

COOKIES

1 large ripe banana

⅓ cup smooth almond butter

3 tablespoons pure maple syrup

½ teaspoon pure vanilla extract

½ teaspoon almond extract

½ cup plain hemp protein powder

¼ cup Dutch-process cocoa powder

1 cup old-fashioned rolled oats

½ teaspoon salt

1 Preheat the oven to 350°F and line a baking sheet with parchment paper.

2 Combine the topping ingredients in a small, shallow bowl.

3 Make the cookies: In a large bowl, mash together the banana, almond butter, maple syrup, vanilla, and almond extract until smooth. Stir in the hemp protein powder and cocoa powder until smooth; the mixture will resemble thick chocolate frosting. Fold in the oats and salt. The dough will be sticky; that's okay!

4 Using an ice-cream dipper for the easiest scooping of the sticky dough, or lightly oiling your fingers to shape the dough, drop generous rounded tablespoons into the topping mixture. Roll to coat, then transfer to the prepared baking sheet, leaving 1 inch apart. Gently flatten each cookie to about 1 inch thick. Bake for 12 minutes, or until the bottoms are lightly browned. Let cool completely before storing loosely covered.

CHOCOLATE CHIP NINJA COOKIES

BRP

MAKES: ABOUT 2 DOZEN COOKIES
TIME: 30 MINUTES, NOT INCLUDING COOLING TIME

Coconut oil, for pan (optional)

½ cup whole wheat white flour

½ cup whole wheat pastry flour

⅓ cup brown rice protein powder

½ teaspoon baking powder

½ teaspoon salt

¼ cup plain unsweetened soy milk

1 tablespoon ground flaxseeds

½ cup coconut sugar or organic dark brown sugar

¼ cup olive or canola oil

¼ cup coconut oil, softened

2 teaspoons pure vanilla extract

⅔ cup vegan chocolate chips

These are undoubtedly cookies: not scones, not drops, not squishy nutty chewy mounds (don't hate; I bake those things, too). Full of chocolate chips in buttery brown sugar dough—without the butter, of course—these have just enough protein in them to make you feel a touch self-righteous about your choice of dessert.

1 Preheat the oven to 350°F. Lightly grease two medium-size baking sheets or line with parchment paper.

2 In a medium-size bowl, sift together the flours, rice protein powder, baking powder, and salt.

3 In a large bowl, with an electric mixer, on high speed, beat together the soy milk and ground flaxseeds. Beat in the coconut sugar, olive oil, coconut oil, and vanilla until smooth. Now use a rubber spatula to fold in the dry mixture and the chocolate chips and mix just enough to moisten and create a soft dough.

4 Scoop the dough with a mechanical cookie scoop onto the prepared baking sheets, about 2 inches apart. Lightly oil your palm and gently press down on each cookie to flatten them slightly.

5 Bake for 10 to 11 minutes, or until the cookies are golden and browned on the bottom. Remove from the oven and let cool on the cookie sheets for a few minutes, then use a spatula to carefully transfer to cooling racks to completely cool. Store loosely covered.

CHOCOLATE CHOCOLATE NINJA COOKIES

Because saying "chocolate" once is never enough.

- ⅓ cup whole wheat white flour
- ⅓ cup whole wheat pastry flour
- ⅓ cup brown rice protein powder
- ⅓ cup Dutch-process cocoa powder
- ½ teaspoon baking powder
- ½ teaspoon salt
- ⅓ cup plain unsweetened soy milk
- 2 tablespoons ground flaxseeds
- ½ cup coconut sugar or organic dark brown sugar
- ¼ cup olive or canola oil
- ¼ cup coconut oil, softened
- 2 teaspoons pure vanilla extract
- ⅔ cup vegan chocolate chips

Follow instructions for the regular chocolate chip cookies, adding the cocoa powder along with the remainder of the dry ingredients.

continued

OATMEAL CHOCOLATE CHUNK COOKIES

Oatmeal and chocolate. Nature's finest combination. It's fine if you disagree because I'll just help myself to another, thanks.

- ⅔ cup whole wheat pastry flour or gluten-free flour mix
- ⅓ cup brown rice protein powder
- ½ teaspoon ground cinnamon
- ½ teaspoon baking powder
- ½ teaspoon salt
- ½ cup plain unsweetened soy milk
- 2 tablespoons ground flaxseeds
- ⅔ cup coconut sugar
- ¼ cup olive or canola oil
- ¼ cup coconut oil, softened
- 1½ teaspoons pure vanilla extract
- 1½ cups old-fashioned rolled oats (certified gluten-free if it matters)
- 2 ounces vegan bitter chocolate, roughly chopped

Follow the instructions for regular chocolate chip cookies, folding in the oats and chopped chocolate after combining the wet and dry ingredients.

PISTACHIO CRANBERRY AVOCADO SOFTIES

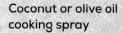

HPP

MAKES: ABOUT 2 DOZEN COOKIES
TIME: 30 MINUTES, NOT INCLUDING COOLING TIME

First I gave you chewies, now I'm getting soft. I blame avocados this time: This wonderful substitute for fat in baked goods makes everything tender, moist, and green. The flavor and texture of these plump, nutty cookies bedazzled with dried cranberries improves as they cool, so do try and leave them alone for at least 15 minutes after baking.

1 Preheat the oven to 350°F and line cookie sheets with parchment paper. Lightly spray the parchment paper with cooking oil spray (the dough is stickier than regular cookie dough and needs a little extra grease). In a small dish, combine the chopped pistachios and hemp seeds.

2 In a glass measuring cup, whisk together the hemp milk and ground flaxseeds and set aside for 2 minutes. Meanwhile, in a large mixing bowl, using an electric mixer on high speed, beat together the mashed avocado and coconut sugar until creamy and as smooth as possible. Beat in the flax mixture, then the vanilla and almond extracts. Add the flour, hemp protein powder, baking soda, and salt and beat until just combined.

continued ➲

Coconut or olive oil cooking spray

½ cup shelled pistachios, finely chopped

2 tablespoons shelled hemp seeds

⅓ cup vanilla almond or hemp milk

2 tablespoons ground flaxseeds

1 cup mashed, ripe avocado (about 1 large Haas avocado)

⅔ cup blond coconut sugar

1 teaspoon pure vanilla extract

1 teaspoon almond extract

1 cup whole wheat pastry flour

⅓ cup unflavored hemp protein powder

½ teaspoon baking soda

½ teaspoon salt

½ cup dried cranberries

SWEET TREATS

3 Use a rubber spatula to fold the cranberries and 2 tablespoons of the pistachio mixture into the dough. Use a mechanical cookie dough scoop to scoop the dough into balls on the prepared cookie sheets, about 2 inches apart. Sprinkle the top of the balls with the remaining pistachio mixture. Or if you're feeling like getting down and dirty, drop the top of each dough ball into the mixture. Lightly oiling your fingers can help things from getting too sticky.

4 Bake for 10 to 12 minutes, or until the cookies are golden and browned on the bottom. Remove from the oven and let cool on the cookie sheets for 2 minutes, then use a spatula to carefully transfer to wire racks to completely cool. Store loosely covered.

PRO-TIP: *For best results, use an avocado that's just turned ripe. You want the flesh to be firm and bright green with little or no brown striations, which can add bitterness. If you're feeling lazy, squish the avocado halves in your hands directly into the mixing bowl, instead of bothering with mashing them in a separate bowl first.*

CRUNCHY NUTTY PEANUT BUTTER HEMP COOKIES

MAKES: 1 DOZEN BIG COOKIES
TIME: 30 MINUTES, NOT INCLUDING COOLING TIME

These are unapologetically boss peanut butter cookies, just sweet enough, wholesome with rolled oats and a touch of whole-grain flour, and munchy-crunchy topped with salted peanuts. Pressing the dough into muffin tins creates pleasingly symmetrical, thick cookies that can easily cradle a big spoonful of your favorite jam. And confuse everyone when you announce you're baking cookies and ask to borrow their muffin tin. Fun!

1 Preheat the oven to 350°F and lightly oil a 12-cup muffin tin.

2 In a mixing bowl, with an electric mixer, on high speed, beat together the peanut butter, coconut oil, sugars, soy milk, and vanilla until smooth. In a separate bowl, mix together the oats, flours, hemp protein powder, and salt. Stir into the peanut butter mixture a few batches at a time to moisten all the ingredients.

3 Divide the dough equally among the muffin cups, pressing the dough evenly into each cup. Press chopped peanuts into the top of each cookie. Bake the cookies for 12 to 15 minutes, or until the cookies are firm and slightly golden. Remove from the oven and let cool for 5 minutes, then carefully remove each cookie and transfer to a rack to cool completely. Store in a loosely covered container.

continued ➲

Coconut or olive oil cooking spray, for muffin tin

½ cup natural peanut butter, smooth or chunky

⅓ cup refined coconut oil, softened

½ cup organic dark brown sugar

⅓ cup organic sugar

½ cup unsweetened soy milk

2 teaspoons pure vanilla extract

1½ cups old-fashioned rolled oats

¾ cup unbleached all-purpose flour

½ cup whole wheat pastry flour

⅓ cup plain hemp protein powder

¾ teaspoon salt

½ cup salted roasted peanuts, roughly chopped

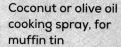

COCONUT-SWEETENED PEANUT BUTTER HEMP COOKIES

Replace both sugars with light brown coconut sugar.

THUMBPRINT PEANUT BUTTER HEMP COOKIES

Press a shallow dent into the top of each cookie before baking, then spoon about a tablespoon of jam (raspberry or strawberry always works) into each indentation before baking.

Chocolate Chip Ninja Cookies, page 204;
Crunchy Nutty Peanut Butter Hemp Cookies, page 209

NO-BAKE SWEET & SALTY GRANOLA BARS

HPP   NSP

MAKES: 16 BARS FOR REGULAR PEOPLE
OR 8 FOR GRANOLA BAR FREAKS
TIME: 30 MINUTES, NOT INCLUDING CHILLING TIME

2 tablespoons refined organic coconut oil, plus more for pan and handling dough

¾ cup brown rice syrup

½ cup pure maple syrup

¼ teaspoon pure vanilla extract

¼ teaspoon sea salt

3 cups old-fashioned rolled oats

1 cup crispy brown rice cereal

½ cup slivered, toasted almonds or roasted walnut pieces

⅔ cup hemp protein powder

1 teaspoon ground cinnamon

½ cup finely chopped dried fruit, such as raisins or dried cranberries

(continued)

Big Granola called me crazy. You can't fit all these things in a granola bar, they said. You can't fight the Granola Bar Mass Industrial Complex, they said. You are delusional and paranoid, they said. Well, let's prove them wrong!

These bars are perfect for when your oven is broken and/or you're living off the grid in an underground bunker to escape Big Granola and/or you don't feel like turning on the oven. Brown rice syrup and maple syrup together make this bar sweet but not cloying, and a flourish of crunchy Maldon sea salt flakes make that sweet and salty thing happen. No fancy Maldon? Then use a little less kosher salt.

1 Line a 9 x 13-inch baking pan with foil and spray or rub the foil with a little coconut oil.

2 In a large saucepan, bring the brown rice syrup and maple syrup to a rapid boil. The bubbling syrups will crawl up the sides of the pan, so make sure to use a large saucepan (2-quart works fine). Boil for about 2 minutes, then lower the heat to low and simmer for another 5 minutes. Turn off the heat and whisk in the coconut oil, vanilla, and salt.

3 In a very large mixing bowl, combine the oats, crispy brown rice, almonds, hemp protein powder, cinnamon, and dried fruit. Pour in the syrup mixture and use a silicone spatula to thoroughly stir the syrup into the dry ingredients. Stir for about 2 minutes; you want to make sure everything is completely coated in sticky syrup.

4 Transfer the mixture to the prepared pan. Lightly oil your fingers with coconut oil and pat the mixture into an even layer in the pan. Immediately sprinkle the toppings evenly over the bars, ending with the Maldon salt, and then very firmly press down over the entire surface of the bars. Make sure to work all the way around the edges of the pan. Move the pan into the fridge for at least 30 minutes to completely chill.

5 To cut the bars, lift the entire sheet of the cookie slab by grabbing the edges of the foil and lifting it out of the pan. Place a cutting board on top of the slab, flip over, and peel away the foil. Flip onto another cutting board and slice into sixteen or eight bars. Store in a lightly covered container, preferably chilled, and for best flavor eat within a week of the collapse of Western civilization.

TOPPING

2 tablespoons shelled hemp seeds

2 tablespoons goji berries

2 tablespoons cacao nibs

2 tablespoons roasted pepitas

½ teaspoon Maldon or similar large-flake sea salt

FROZEN AVOCADO PUDDING PROTEIN CHEESECAKES

MAKES: 12 MINI CHEESECAKES OR 1 (8- TO 9-INCH) PIE
TIME: ABOUT 1 HOUR, INCLUDING FREEZING TIME

Healthy, protein packin', little frozen cheesecake. Do I need to say anything else? If a bunch of little single-serving cheesecakes make you question and stress out about what else you'll be eating for the next twelve days, you can always press the crust into a regular 8- to 10-inch lightly oiled springform pan and pour in the filling, freeze, and be faced with just one big cake instead.

1 Make the chocolate ganache topping first: In a small saucepan, bring the almond milk to a rolling boil. Turn off the heat, add the chocolate chips and coconut oil, and stir consistently until completely melted and silky smooth. Cover and set aside for now.

2 Make the crust: Line a 12-cup muffin tin with paper liners. Spray the liners with coconut oil cooking spray.

3 In a blender, pulse together the granola and coconut oil into fine crumbs. Divide the mixture evenly in the oiled paper liners and press down the crumbs evenly on the bottom of each liner.

4 Make the filling: Rinse and dry the blender. Pulse together the coconut milk, chia seeds, lemon juice, coconut sugar, rice protein powder, vanilla, almond extract, and salt for at least a minute, until very smooth.

continued ➲

CHOCOLATE GANACHE & SEA SALT CASHEW TOPPING

3 tablespoons almond or coconut milk

3 heaping tablespoons vegan chocolate chips

2 teaspoons coconut oil

½ cup roughly chopped roasted cashews

Generous pinch of sea salt or favorite large-flake salt

CRUST

Coconut cooking oil spray

1 cup *Chocolate Hazelnut Hemp Granola* (page 35) or any vegan granola, homemade or store-bought

1 tablespoon coconut oil, melted

(continued)

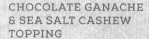

SWEET TREATS

FILLING

¾ cup full-fat Thai coconut milk

2 teaspoons chia seeds, preferably white chia

2 tablespoons freshly squeezed lemon juice

½ cup coconut sugar

¼ cup unflavored brown rice protein or pea protein powder

2 teaspoons pure vanilla extract

½ teaspoon almond extract

¼ teaspoon sea salt

½ frozen ripe avocado

2 frozen ripe bananas

5 Thaw the avocado on the kitchen counter only just enough to soften it up to dice into small pieces. Slice the frozen banana. Add to the blender and pulse only long enough to create a creamy mixture: The idea is to keep the batter still cold.

6 Divide the batter evenly among the crusts in the prepared pan. Top each cake with a dollop of chocolate ganache and use the tip of a chopstick to swirl the chocolate on top. Sprinkle each with some chopped cashews and a pinch of sea salt. Freeze for about an hour until firm. When you're ready to eat, thaw first for 5 to 8 minutes, for best flavor and texture.

GRANOLA & ALMOND BUTTER BAKED APPLES

 HPP NSP

MAKES: 4 STUFFED APPLES
TIME: ABOUT 1 HOUR

Baked apples stuffed with a hearty filling are a standby treat for me during cooler months. This recipe may be in the sweets chapter, but gravitate toward these for breakfast often, or a substantial snack served cold. The combination of melting, tender baked apple and the hemp protein and almond butter filling reminds me just a little of a tiny deconstructed frangipane tart, the classic tart of baked fruit nestled in dense almond paste cus-tard. These are best made with large, firm baking apples, such as Granny Smith, Braeburn, Cortland, or even Fuji.

1 Preheat the oven to 350°F and have ready an 8 x 8-inch baking dish.

2 With a paring knife, remove and discard the core and seeds from the apples but leave the bottom intact.

3 In a small bowl, use a fork to mix together the almond butter, hemp protein, almond milk, maple syrup, and cinnamon.

4 Pack the bottom of each apple with a quarter of the raisins. Firmly pack the almond butter mixture into each apple: Use a spatula or the fork to mash it into the center of each apple and smooth down the top. Place the apples, filling side up, in the baking dish.

continued ➲

4 large baking apples

¼ cup smooth almond butter

¼ cup unflavored or vanilla-flavored hemp protein powder

⅓ cup unsweetened vanilla or plain almond milk

1 tablespoon pure maple syrup

½ teaspoon ground cinnamon

2 tablespoons raisins or dried cranberries

TOPPING

4 heaping tablespoons vegan granola, any kind you like

4 teaspoons pure maple syrup

Ground cinnamon

5 Add your topping: Press 1 tablespoon of granola into the top of each apple. Drizzle 1 teaspoon of maple syrup on each apple, and sprinkle with cinnamon.

6 Cover the dish tightly with foil and bake for 30 minutes, then uncover and bake for another 10 to 15 minutes, or until the apples are very tender and juicy and the skin has split open a little. The apples will be very hot right out of the oven! Either let them stand for at least 5 minutes to cool, or use a serrated knife to slice open before eating, to speed up the cooling process.

ORANGE CREME FROSTYCAKES

MAKES: 12 MINI CHEESECAKES OR 1 (8- TO 9-INCH) PIE
TIME: ABOUT 1 HOUR, INCLUDING FREEZING TIME

Another frozen protein cheesecake, this time swirled with orange and vanilla. A ginger or cinnamon-spice granola is a very good idea for creating the crust, but I can't blame you if you opt for a chocolate granola crust.

COCONUT VANILLA CREME

3 tablespoons full-fat coconut milk

1 tablespoon coconut sugar

½ teaspoon pure vanilla extract

CRUST

Coconut cooking oil spray

1 cup *Trail Mix Protein Granola* (page 37) or any vegan granola, homemade or store-bought

1 tablespoon coconut oil, melted

1 Make the coconut vanilla creme: In a mixing bowl, whisk together the creme ingredients until smooth. Set in the refrigerator to chill until ready to use.

2 Make the crust: Line a 12-cup muffin tin with paper liners. Spray the liners with the cooking spray. In a blender, pulse together the granola and coconut oil into fine crumbs. Divide the mixture evenly among the oiled paper liners and press down the crumbs evenly on the bottom of each liner.

3 Make the filling: Rinse and dry the blender. Pulse together the coconut milk, chia seeds, orange juice and zest, coconut sugar, pea protein powder, vanilla and almond extracts, turmeric, and salt for at least a minute, until very smooth.

4 Thaw the avocado on the kitchen counter only just enough to soften it up to peel and dice into small pieces. Slice the frozen banana. Add to the blender and pulse just long enough to create a creamy mixture: The idea is to keep the mixture cold.

5 Divide the banana mixture evenly among the crusts in the prepared pan. Top each cake with a dollop of coconut vanilla creme and use the tip of a chopstick to swirl the topping in a pretty pattern. Freeze for about an hour, until firm. When you're ready to eat, thaw first for 5 to 8 minutes, for best flavor and texture.

FILLING

¾ cup full-fat Thai coconut milk

2 teaspoons chia seeds, preferably white chia

1 large, juicy orange, peeled, seeded, and chopped

½ teaspoon grated orange zest

½ cup coconut sugar

¼ cup unflavored pea protein powder

2 teaspoons pure vanilla extract

½ teaspoon almond extract

½ teaspoon ground turmeric

¼ teaspoon sea salt

½ frozen ripe avocado, slightly thawed

2 frozen ripe bananas, sliced

CASHEW GINGER RICE PUDDING

PPP or BRP NSP

MAKES: 4 CUPS PUDDING

TIME: ABOUT 45 MINUTES, NOT INCLUDING WHERE OR HOW YOU GOT THAT LEFTOVER RICE

- ¾ cup unroasted cashew pieces
- 3 tablespoons shelled hemp seeds
- 2½ cups hot water
- ¾ cup coconut sugar
- ⅓ cup unflavored pea or brown rice protein powder
- 1 teaspoon pure vanilla extract
- 1 teaspoon ground ginger
- 1 teaspoon ground cinnamon, plus more for garnish
- Big pinch of ground cloves
- ½ teaspoon salt
- 2 cups cold, cooked basmati brown or white rice
- ½ cup raisins or chopped dried fruit
- ¼ cup diced candied ginger

Just rice pudding? How dare you?! Rice pudding is perfection, a treat that feels like a meal that's better as a substantial sweet snack than a dessert. This one is all dressed up with Indian-inspired flavors, but don't miss out on the comforting simplicity of the basic but not boring variation at the end.

1 Soak the cashews, hemp seeds, and hot water together for 20 minutes. I do this directly in the blender jar because . . .

2 Once the cashews have softened up, add the coconut sugar, pea protein powder, vanilla, ground ginger, cinnamon, cloves, and salt. Pulse until very smooth.

3 Pour the mixture into a large saucepan and add the rice, raisins, and candied ginger. Bring the mixture to an active simmer over medium heat, stirring the pudding constantly with a wooden spoon; the cashew milk will thicken as it cooks, so it's important to keep stirring to prevent burning.

4 Cook, stirring, for 8 to 10 minutes, or until the pudding reaches your desired thick consistency. Remove from the heat and ladle into either individual parfait cups or one large glass dish. Sprinkle the top with a little ground cinnamon. Cover and chill for at least 10 minutes to cool the pudding and let it set a little.

PURE & SIMPLE CASHEW RICE PUDDING

Use organic sugar in place of coconut sugar.

Keep the vanilla extract, but leave out the ginger, cinnamon, cloves, candied ginger, and raisins.

I know I just said leave out the cinnamon, but add a light dusting of ground cinnamon on top of each serving for that classic look.

THANKS *and* ACKNOWLEDGMENTS

The directions for creating almost any cookbook are at their core the same, every time, every book: cook, shop, write, re-write, cook again, write again, bake for a few months (weeks!) as it goes into production, and then serve to a (hopefully) hungry public.

The ingredients, however, shift with each preparation. And the most important ingredients of all are the people in your life that help you, humble cook & author, hold it all together through the often slapdash process of bringing a jumble of recipes, photos, and words to life. Some of these "ingredients" are reliable, tested favorites, others are delightful new additions, and none are optional. Thank you, friends.

John Stavropoulos, partner in endless grocery shopping and dish duty crimes

Timberly Stephens, number 1 recipe development ninja lieutenant kung lentil loaf scone gravy biscuit fu master

Isa Chandra Moskowitz, cue the flashback of us as young cookbook punks in training

Vanessa Rees, my always evolving and kickass food photographer and stylist and her hardcore backup crew: Rachel Rees, Mélanie, Sophie, and Linda

Teresa (mom) and Nerio (dad)

My baddass, multi-skilled editor Renee Sedilar and the super ninja clan team at DaCapo

Christine E. Marra at *Marrathon Editorial*, always running never sleeping

Ellen Brown, recipe tester pro to the rescue

My wise sensei and agent Marc Gerald and The Agency

And of course a lovable but not to be messed with ninja clan. Some have written or tested the contents of this book, others baked or let me take over their kitchen, and almost everyone listened to me endlessly emote during this trying and protein-loaded time of cookbook creation: Jacob Landrau & Dawn Slawta-Landrau (invading their secluded forest home kitchen one protein recipe session at a time), Adam Leibling (evil ghost ninja writer nemesis), Abby Wohl (sister from another mother), Russel Heiman, Dawne Eng, Mike Townsed, Josh Notjosh, Shimmie Vegan, Rachel McCrystal and the Woodstock Farm Animal Sanctuary family, Ian Miller and Tracy Miller, my Vegan Mashup family (Betsy Carson, Toni Fiore, Miyoko Schinner), Sam Lerner, Nick Turner, Luke Crane, and my family at Kickstarter.

METRIC CONVERSIONS

- The recipes in this book have not been tested with metric measurements, so some variations might occur.

- Remember that the weight of dry ingredients varies according to the volume or density factor: 1 cup of flour weighs far less than 1 cup of sugar, and 1 tablespoon doesn't necessarily hold 3 teaspoons.

GENERAL FORMULA FOR METRIC CONVERSION

Ounces to grams	ounces × 28.35 = grams
Grams to ounces	grams × 0.035 = ounces
Pounds to grams	pounds × 453.5 = grams
Pounds to kilograms	pounds × 0.45 = kilograms
Cups to liters	cups × 0.24 = liters
Fahrenheit to Celsius	(°F – 32) × 5 ÷ 9 = °C
Celsius to Fahrenheit	(°C × 9) ÷ 5 + 32 = °F

VOLUME (LIQUID) MEASUREMENTS

1 teaspoon = ⅙ fluid ounce = 5 milliliters

1 tablespoon = ½ fluid ounce = 15 milliliters

2 tablespoons = 1 fluid ounce = 30 milliliters

¼ cup = 2 fluid ounces = 60 milliliters

⅓ cup = 2⅔ fluid ounces = 79 milliliters

½ cup = 4 fluid ounces = 118 milliliters

1 cup or ½ pint = 8 fluid ounces = 250 milliliters

2 cups or 1 pint = 16 fluid ounces = 500 milliliters

4 cups or 1 quart = 32 fluid ounces = 1,000 milliliters

1 gallon = 4 liters

VOLUME (DRY) MEASUREMENTS

¼ teaspoon = 1 milliliter

½ teaspoon = 2 milliliters

¾ teaspoon = 4 milliliters

1 teaspoon = 5 milliliters

1 tablespoon = 15 milliliters

¼ cup = 59 milliliters

⅓ cup = 79 milliliters

½ cup = 118 milliliters

⅔ cup = 158 milliliters

¾ cup = 177 milliliters

1 cup = 225 milliliters

4 cups or 1 quart = 1 liter

½ gallon = 2 liters

1 gallon = 4 liters

OVEN TEMPERATURE EQUIVALENTS, FAHRENHEIT (F) AND CELSIUS (C)

100°F = 38°C

200°F = 95°C

250°F = 120°C

300°F = 150°C

350°F = 180°C

400°F = 205°C

450°F = 230°C

WEIGHT (MASS) MEASUREMENTS

1 ounce = 30 grams

2 ounces = 55 grams

3 ounces = 85 grams

4 ounces = ¼ pound = 125 grams

8 ounces = ½ pound = 240 grams

12 ounces = ¾ pound = 375 grams

16 ounces = 1 pound = 454 grams

LINEAR MEASUREMENTS

½ in = 1½ cm

1 inch = 2½ cm

6 inches = 15 cm

8 inches = 20 cm

10 inches = 25 cm

12 inches = 30 cm

20 inches = 50 cm

INDEX